# How to Teach Debating:

# Theory & Practical Handbook for the Non-Native Teacher, Debate Coach & International English Language Learner Worldwide

## Thomas Jerome Baker

Thomas Jerome Baker

# How to Teach Debating

# DEDICATION

"It was the best of times, it was the worst of times..." ~ Charles Dickens, "*A Tale of Two Cities*"

In the quotation above we find a contradiction. How can the "best" be the "worst"? Likewise, most debate coaches have differing interpretations about debating. As a debate coach, I emphasize the practical, namely, you learn to debate, by debating.

I dedicate this book to all teachers, coaches, and students worldwide, and especially to the non-native speaker of English. Since most books on debating are aimed at native speakers of English, this book addresses this disparity while still being useful to a native speaker.

For example, there are many drills and exercises. This makes it a highly practical book for the non-native speaker, who above all else, will benefit most from such practice. Nonetheless, it also addresses debating theory. Therefore, it is an excellent resource book to have.

Finally, debating helps you to understand that others see the world differently. This understanding promotes mutual respect and tolerance of diversity. In this way, debate plays a role in building a better world for everyone to live in...

**Thomas Jerome Baker,**

**Santiago de Chile,**

**November 1, 2013**

# How to Teach Debating

# CONTENTS

# ACKNOWLEDGMENTS

This book is because of my wife Gabriela, and my son, Thomas Jerome Baker, Jr. I owe you both an absolute debt of gratitude for your inspiration.

It is you two who provide the impetus for me to write, again, and yet again. Thank you.

I love you both more than words will ever express.

# PROLOGUE

"Sooner or later all the people of the world will have to discover a way to live together in peace... If this is to be achieved, man must evolve for all human conflict a method which rejects revenge, aggression, and retaliation..." ~ Dr. Martin Luther King, Jr., 1964 Nobel Peace Prize Acceptance Speech, (Source: Nobel Prize.org) http://bit.ly/15tnJdb   http://bit.ly/13TaO8r

The ability to disagree, without being disagreeable, to have respect for, and tolerance of, people who do not share our opinions, is a fundamental aspect of debating. In this sense, Dr. King would most likely approve of debating. It has the potential to achieve peace and understanding between the people and nations of the world. This is the transformative power of debating: it can truly make Dr. King's "Dream" of peaceful coexistence a reality.

**What Is Debate?**

The human body is made of flesh, blood, and bones - we are fragile. Man was not created for conflict; man was not built for battle. On the contrary, as Ghandi put it, "an eye for an eye will make the whole world blind". One way to avoid such an outcome is by learning to debate with people with whom you disagree.

1

Thus, debating can promote constructive dialogue, which in turn reduces the likelihood of destructive wars. From this perspective, "debate" can be broadly defined as a method of peaceful conflict resolution. While peace is desirable, are there any other reasons to teach students to debate? My answer: "Yes".

## Why Debate?

First of all, debate is fun. It is a social activity that requires cooperation and collaboration with teammates. Activities such as doing research, exchanging ideas, preparing speeches, practicing drills, speaking in public, and listening to the opinions of others are all ways in which the social aspects of debate are evident. Moreover, through debate, we meet new people; we make new friends; we enrich our lives in many profound and diverse ways.

Secondly, debate is for everyone. Tall or short, rich or poor, male or female, young or old, black or white, left or right; debate is for all of us. Debate is about all people getting their opportunity, equally, to voice their opinions, to advocate for change. In this sense, debate makes no demand on its participants other than a willingness to share their opinions with others. The chances of winning, or losing, are equal. Winners learn to be humble and modest in victory, in defeat we learn grace, and we resolve to do better the next time.

Thirdly, debate teaches critical thinking skills. We analyse arguments to determine: if there are problems with the reasoning used, if there are inconsistencies or contradictions, if there are irrelevant points being made, if there are sources used that are authoritative or not, etc. We examine an issue from a number of angles, do research, discuss our positions with others, determine the content and strategy of our speeches, and ultimately, stand in front of an audience to try to persuade them of the rightness and righteousness of our positions. Again, all of these activities promote critical thinking.

Fourthly, debate helps EFL students to develop their listening, reading, writing, speaking, and research skills. All of these skills are used, in an integrated manner, to participate successfully in debate. This means that students are learning to find, analyse, synthesize, prepare, and deliver the most favorable material possible to support and/or defend their positions. These skills can be collectively termed "communication skills".

Fifthly, debate experience helps prepare debaters for success in their future careers. For example, in the USA, more than half the members of Congress have high school or college debate experience. This includes most Presidents and Supreme Court Justices. Furthermore, it is a well-known fact that employers value communication skills. Thus, it is little wonder that oral job interviews are conducted for most job opportunities nowadays.

Finally, debate is a powerful force for positive transformation in our lives. It allows us not only to criticise the things about our world that we don't like or don't agree with. We can also propose ways in which improvements could be made.

For instance, this could be at home with rules that we think are unfair; at school with regulations that seem unjust; in our community regarding issues such as transportation, sanitation, etc.; in our country regarding poverty, security, etc.; or global issues such as human rights, terrorism, global warming, AIDS, genocide, etc. In conclusion, debate empowers us to change the world for the better.

\*\*

# PART ONE:
# SNAPSHOTS OF DEBATE

In this section there are snapshots, literally and figuratively speaking, that represent the recent history of debate in Chile. Although great care has been taken to select debates that collectively tell a unified story, no claim can be made for completeness. Each snapshot is taken from a particular instance of a debating competition in the years from 2002 – 2009.

The aim is to give the reader a view of debate from the perspective of a time traveler. You travel "back to the future", from debate to debate, with a knowledgeable friend, the author of this book. Together, we become "members of the audience". After having "attended" four debates, you, dear friend, will have inductively gained, not only a working knowledge of different forms of debate competition, but an understanding of debate itself.

\*\*

# CHAPTER 1
# MELIPILLA 2002

We travel back in time to Thursday, November 28, 2002. We are at Escuela República de Brasil in Melipilla to attend the Regional Semi-Final Debate Competition for school children ages 10-12. We park and hurry to our seats, arriving just in time to hear the Head Teacher announce the motion:

"Pregnant students should be allowed to stay in their regular schools".

A quick look at the young debaters shows they are nervous but eager to begin the debate. An eyewitness account is provided by Dr. Alfred (Tuna) Snider, an internationally renowned expert on debates, who is present in the audience today:

"There were a series of six speeches, three by each side, with each speech lasting two minutes. After these constructive speeches there would be a brief conference for the teams to plan strategy, and then three, two-minute speeches by each side. Thus, each debate took about 50 minutes.

The **proposition** team argued that pregnant students were not criminals and should not be discriminated against.

The **opposition** team argued that the students would be embarrassed and teased by others, that the desks and chairs were not suitable, and that there might be accidents threatening the safety of the children. The conference came and the students spoke to each other enthusiastically.

Then we heard the remaining speeches where they attacked and defended the various issues in the debate. After each speaker there was a round of applause, and a big applause at the end."

As we leave the debate, we pause for a moment in the bright sunshine. Off to our left,    we can see the four proud teams who debated today are taking photos with Dr. Snider:

**

# CHAPTER 2:
# VALPARAÍSO 2005

Our time travels take us forward to December 7, 2005.  We have arrived at the "Congreso Nacional" in Valparaíso, Chile.  We are just in time to hear Ubaldo Nadalini from the Programa Inglés Abre Puertas (English Opens Doors Program) announce:

Ubaldo Nadalini: *"Dear students, now we begin today's final competition. Comenzaremos la competencia del debate. In which the winning team from the Metropolitan Region will face the*

*winning team of the Fifth Region. We now call the participants to approach and have their seats. Llamamos los participantes acercarse y tomar asiento.*

*From Instituto del Puerto de San Antonio (polite applause) we gladly welcome students: José Amestica, Alán Gomez, David Vergara, Felipe Reis, Claudio Diaz, y Felipe Diaz, and of course, greetings to the teacher, Ms. Irene Castro, and the Principal of the institution, Father José Antonio Lopez. Please have your seats."* (pause)

Ubaldo pauses as the debaters take their seats, then continues: *"From Benjamín Vicuña High School, Liceo Benjamín Vicuña de La Florida, we gladly welcome students: María Jesús Martinez, Claudia Adonis - fuerte aplauso – Maciel Salpato, Andrés Finchi, Simón Veloso, y Evelyn Medina. And of course, y por supuesto saludamos al profesor, Señor Julio Pérez. Y al Director del establecimiento, el Señor Rubén Catalán.*

**Liceo Vicuña Mackenna**

The Motion is read: "Should developed nations cancel the debt of poor countries?"

After a hard fought debate, the audience waits on the judges' decision. Interestingly enough, among the judges are the ambassadors from the United States, Canada, and England. This is quite a distinguished panel of judges indeed. Finally, the decision is announced: The winner is: Instituto del Puerto de San Antonio!

\*\*

# CHAPTER 3:
# SANTIAGO, OCTOBER 2009

Leaving Valparaíso, we travel to Santiago, arriving at *Facultad de Economía y Negocios de la Universidad de Chile*. The date is Friday, October 2, 2009. Today, Colegio Santa Emilia de Antofagasta is trying to win the National Debating Championship for the second consecutive year. They are the **opposition** team in this debate and Instituto Comercial Osorno is the **proposition** team. The Motion for today is: "This house believes that voting should be compulsory." I ask myself, "Will there be a new national champion today?"

Instituto Comercial Osorno begins the debate with a very solid performance from the opening speaker. He has "ticked all of the boxes", which means that the first speaker has done all the things that a good first speaker should do: Greet the members of the jury, the audience, the opposing team; introduce himself and his teammates; define the terms of the debate; preview his teams' arguments; and make his argument for compulsory voting.

"That was a solid performance", I think to myself. I watch the first speaker from the opposition team take the floor and repeat the performance, "ticking all of the boxes". Then something unexpected happens. The first speaker asks the audience to vote. Turning to the Osorno team, looking them in the eyes, she says, "I noticed you didn't vote. Evidently you don't like being told to vote, but you think it's OK for everyone else".

My jaw drops open, along with everyone else's in the audience. I think to myself: "That was a brilliant bit of strategy, and unless Osorno can rebut that immediately, this debate is over." Will Osorno's second speaker be able to react with an effective rebuttal?

I watch as Osorno's second speaker gives his prepared speech – no rebuttal. In effect, Osorno has been made to look like a bunch of hypocrites – advocating one thing for everyone else while doing another thing themselves. If the rebuttal is delayed until the summary speech, it will be too late. Why? The judges' minds will already be made up.

Finally, the summary speaker for Osorno does make an impassioned rebuttal, but it's too little, too late. Everyone in the audience waits on the judges' decision, but absolutely noone is surprised when the announcement is made: Colegio Santa Emilia de Antofagasta has won the National Debating Championship for the second consecutive year! http://bit.ly/12SQixe

http://www.ustream.tv/recorded/2266985

\*\*

**Final Debate: Qatar 2009 – Chile VS New Zealand**

Finally, we make our longest travel, making a final stop in the Middle East. We are in Doha, the capital of Qatar, and the date is November 5, 2009. The Chilean National High School debating team is debating New Zealand, the reigning World Schools Debate Champions.

This is the championship debate of the Mini-World Schools Debating Championships (WSDC), a preparatory tournament for the 2010 WSDC. Teams from all over the world are here: Chile, New Zealand, the USA, Qatar, China, Bosnia & Herzegovina, Sudan, Oman, Uganda, United Arab Emirates, and Lebanon.

Chile's very presence in the championship debate is improbable, a true Cinderella story. Chile first competed in WSDC in January 2009, for the very first time, in Greece. Although Chile finished in last place, the experience was beneficial. Here in Qatar, this is only Chile's _second_ international competition.

New Zealand, the proposition team, is made up of James Penn, Nicholas Orr, and Tim Robinson. Chile, the opposition team, is made up of Domingo Carbone, Paulina Valenzuela, and Valentina Salvatierra. Nicolás Sandoval and Sofia Bernier are alternates, because WSDC rules allow only 3 speakers per team, although WSDC debates consist of four speeches.

Team Chile is coached by Alvaro Ferrer and Catalina Bascur. The team is sponsored by Universidad Andrés Bello and the English Speaking Union of Chile.

The debate is being judged by *nine* judges. They are Loke Wing Fatt (Singapore), Sue Edwards (Qatar), Piyanart Faktorngpan (Thailand), Debbie Newman (England), Joseph Agula (Uganda), Greg Paulk (USA), Tang Neng (China), Sam Greenland (Hong Kong), and Simon Quinn (Australia).

The Motion is announced:

"This house believes that a country should not punish those who pay bribes to officials of other countries."

Team New Zealand, the **proposition** team, speaks first. Team Chile, the **opposition** team, speaks second. The teams take turns speaking, proposition then opposition, with each of the first three speakers on each team speaking for **8** minutes. For the final summary speech, which lasts only **4** minutes, the opposition –

Chile, speaks *first* and the proposition team, New Zealand, speaks *last*, closing the debate. The WSDC rules allow either the first or second speaker on a team to make the final summary speech – the third speaker can not make the summary speech.

The reason that the opposition team makes the final summary speech **first** is that throughout the debate they have enjoyed the advantage of speaking after the proposition team – which makes it easy to rebut the proposition arguments.

By making the opposition team give their final summary speech first, the advantage enjoyed by the opposition team, throughout the debate, is equalized.

In WSDC style, the first three speakers on each team must answer at least 2 questions, called Point of Information (POI). The POI may be asked after the first minute and up until the seventh minute. The first minute and the last minute are "protected" from questions.

To ask a POI, any member of the opposite team stands and says, "Point of Information." The speaker may decide to accept or refuse the POI by saying either "Yes" to accept the question or "No thank you" to refuse it.

All debaters must try to make a POI, regardless of whether it is accepted or not. Again, the only requirement is that a minimum of two POI's be accepted by each speaker. If a speaker does not accept 2 POIs, there is a penalty.

What about the debate? Who won? The nine judges made a unanimous decision, voting the debate 9-0. Such a result is extremely rare. It means that the winner thoroughly dominated the debate in all its aspects, in all its phases. Who won? Chile won! Debating in Chile has come a long way baby...Watch the debate here: http://vimeo.com/7490164

# REVIEW & DISCUSSION

Was the debate in Melipilla in Spanish or in English? Support your answer.

How old were the debaters in Melipilla?

Do you think the debate topic was appropriate? Why or why not?

Who were the two teams who debated in Valparaíso?

What was special about three of the judges in Valparaíso?

What do you think the judges look for in a good debater?

What was the specific location in Valparaíso where the debate was held?

Why do you think the announcer, Ubaldo Nadalini, spoke "Spanglish"?

Who were the two teams who debated in Santiago?

What was Colegio Santa Emilia's surprise opening strategy?

Can you explain why rebuttal of all arguments should be done in every speech?

Can you explain why Team Chile was successful in Qatar?

Can you explain the way the championship debate in Qatar was conducted?

What is a "Point of Information"?

How much time do you have to ask a POI:
a. 10 seconds,  or    b. 1 minute

Compare and contrast the WSDC debating style & the style used in Melipilla.

Is it easier to be the proposition or the opposition team? Defend your answer.

Is it enough for the opposition to just prove that the proposition team is wrong?

Is it enough for the proposition to just prove they are right? Explain your answers.

Predict the future of debating in Chile – bigger & better or smaller & worse?  Why?  Explain your prediction.

In your opinion, what is the biggest obstacle to the widespread use of debate as a teaching and learning tool for English Language Learners?

**

# PART TWO:

# THE BASICS

In this section, we will go over the three basic elements of debate. These are the motion, the proposition, and the opposition. In a debate; we need a controversial topic, a team who is in favor of the topic, and a team who is against the topic. A series of quotes will illustrate these basic elements as we begin to learn more about debate:

**Abraham Lincoln**: "When I am getting ready to reason with a man, I spend one-third of my time thinking about myself and what I am going to say; and two-thirds of my time thinking about him and what he is going to say."

**Margaret Thatcher**: "I love argument, I love debate. I don't expect anyone just to sit there and agree with me..."

**Mark Rutherford**: "There is always a multitude of reasons, both in favor of doing a thing, and against doing it. The art of debate lies in presenting them..."

**Samuel Butler**: "It is not he who gains the exact point in dispute who scores most in controversy - - but he who has shown the better temper."

**Baltasar Gracian**: "Don't take the wrong side of an argument just because your opponent has taken the right side."

\*\*

# CHAPTER 4:

# THE MOTION

The motion, or resolution, is the topic that the debate will be about. It restricts the debate to a specific topic. Judges, the audience, and the opposing team expect the debaters to stick to the topic during the debate. The motion is usually a controversial issue.

The motion must be debatable. For example, the motion, "This House Believes That (THBT) the sun is the center of the universe", is not debatable. There is no controversy, no possibility of two different positions (for / against).

On the other hand, the motion, "THBT voting should be compulsory", is debatable. Here, two different positions (for / against) are possible. Debate is necessary to resolve the dispute.

To begin the debate, each team must **define** the **key terms** in the motion. This is important because it ensures that the debaters have the same understanding of what the motion means. For instance, in the motion, "THBT voting should be compulsory", the key term is, *compulsory.*

It should be defined by both teams, using an authoritative dictionary. If the definitions are contradictory, or a *weird* definition is given by either team, that point should be clarified by the opposite team in the next speech.

In the motion, "THBT voting **should** be compulsory", the verb, **should,** is also important. It indicates that the **staus quo**, or the way things are *now*, are undesirable. Therefore, this is a debate about whether or not a **change** ought to be made in the *future.* For a "status quo" or "change" debate, the proposition team must offer sufficient, clear and compelling reasons and evidence to make the change in the future.

The opposition team, on the other hand, must offer sufficient, clear and compelling reasons and evidence to reject the arguments of the proposition team. The negative team can, either in addition or alternatively, offer a **counter plan**, that is, **agree** with the proposition team that a change needs to be made, **but** offer a **_better plan_** to solve the problem.

To put this in football terms, this is *"playing defense by going on offense"*. In other words, if my team has the ball, your team can't score. Chilean football fans will recognise this strategy as the one used by Marcelo Bielsa to classify Chile for the 2010 World Cup in South Africa. Incidentally, it was used masterfully by Chile's National Debating Team to win the 2009 Mini-WSDC in Qatar. Chile dominated New Zealand, winning a 9-0 decision, an almost unheard of result for a championship debate!

Let's look at another motion, "THBT governments **should** _never_ bail out big companies. What terms need to be defined? *Government, bail out*, and *big companies* all need to be defined. Does "governments" include any representative body, regardless of the level of government (local, state or national) or type of government (dictatorship, communist, etc.)?

What is a *bail out*? Would a bail out include tax incentives or only money given by the government to the big company? Finally, when is a company a *big company*? Is being a big company the only requirement necessary to receive a bail out or are there other conditions that the big company must meet?

This motion seems complicated, doesn't it? First of all, let's do the definitions. According to the 2009 Cambridge Dictionary, a government is defined as, "the system used for controlling a country, city, or group of people". This means that any government, regardless of size or type, is included in the use of the term, government.

"Bail out" is defined by the same dictionary above as, "to help an organization that is in difficulty, usually by giving or lending them money". Therefore, to bail out a big company means either giving or lending them money because they are having financial difficulties.

18

"Big company" is defined by the 2009 Cambridge Dictionary of American English as, "powerful, influential businesses and financial organisations". Therefore, there are two preconditions that a company must meet to be considered big. The company must be powerful and influential. A bank, such as Bank of America, and a company, such as General Motors, both of whom received government bailouts, meet this definition: powerful and influential.

Having defined our key terms, the debate is now able to be interpreted in a **reasonable** manner that permits debate. THBT governments should *never* bail out big companies.This is a status quo / change debate. Paying attention to the word **never,** the proposition team must present sufficient, clear and compelling reasons and evidence to implement this policy in the future. Conversely, the opposition team must present sufficient, clear and compelling reasons and evidence to reject the arguments of the proposition team. Again, alternatively or in addition, a better counter plan could be offered by the opposition team.

Finally, it must be said that the motion should always be interpreted **fairly**. The purpose of the debate is to argue *for* or *against* something. This is expected by the judges, the audience, and the opposing team. To try to define terms in a weird way or interpret the intent of the debate very narrowly in order to gain an advantage in the debate is known as a "**squirrel**".

**Squirreling** in a debate is certain to make the judges angry, and your team will be penalised severely as a result. In the debate, "THBT governments should never bail out big companies", the obvious intent of the motion is to debate recent events in the USA, in which the government bailed out big business and the big banks.

That is the debate that the judges and the audience want to see; depriving them of the pleasure of seeing this debate by squirreling on the definitions would have dire consequences.

\*\*

# CHAPTER 5:

# THE PROPOSITION

The proposition team is the affirmative team. This means they are *for* the motion. The proposition team wins by presenting sufficient, clear and compelling reasons and evidence to the judges and audience. The proposition team needs to follow five guiding principles in building their case:

1. Use the best evidence available. This means evidence that is recent, up-dated, authoritative, free from bias, relevant, verifiable, factual, and acceptable by most people.

2. Use enough evidence to support their case. Each speaker (except for the final summary or reply speaker) should have at least two arguments with analysis in depth that justifies the affirmative case.

3. Relate the evidence clearly to the case you are trying to prove. Here it must be clearly and explicitly stated how the evidence relates to your arguments. Do not expect the judges to assume anything that you don't tell them. This means stating the obvious.

4. Use evidence that can not be questioned or doubted. Make sure the evidence is accurate, that your sources are experts, that your facts and figures contain no errors. Remember, it is your responsibility to check any evidence that someone else on your team provides you with. Above all, never "make up" or "falsify" or "fabricate" fictitious evidence. If you get caught doing this, you and your team will be penalised severely.

5. **Undermine** the opposition arguments. Never ignore your opponents arguments. Clash is a necessary element of debate. Don't get so caught up making your arguments that you forget to point out inconsistencies, mistakes, faulty logic or other problems

in your opponents' arguments, especially if they are making a **counter plan!**

**

# CHAPTER 6:

# THE OPPOSITION

The opposition team is the negative team. This means they are *against* the motion. The opposition team wins by presenting sufficient, clear and compelling reasons and evidence to reject the arguments of the proposition team. The opposition team needs to follow one basic guideline:

**The proposition team is wrong.** The proposition team is **wrong** because:

They are naively optimistic about human nature.
Their evidence is old, out-dated, biased, irrelevant, etc.
Their proposal won't solve the problem.
Their proposal will only make things worse.
Their plan has already been tried and failed.
Their plan is impractical – won't work in the real world.
Their plan costs too much money.
Their plan requires undue suffering, harm, and human sacrifice.
Their conclusions don't follow their evidence.
Their expert is not an expert (Einstein is a genius but not when it comes to drugs, alcohol, love, bail outs, etc.).
You have a counter plan that is bigger, better, more important, more beneficial, etc.

**

**Exercises:**

| MOTION | TERM TO DEFINE |
|---|---|
| THBT marijuana should be legalised. | |
| TH regrets holding the 2008 Olympics in Beijing. | |

Write the terms you would define in the chart.

Are the motions debatable? Why or why not?

Proposition: For each motion above:
Name (3) arguments to support your position.

a. _____

b. _____

c. _____

Opposition: For each motion: You agree with the proposition, but, you have a counter plan that is bigger / better / more important / cheaper / more beneficial, etc.

Counter Plan:

_____

Proposition: Why is the opposition counter plan wrong?

The opposition is wrong <u>because</u> **they say**

_____

but **we say** _____

**therefore** _____ .

---

# PART 3:

# SKILLS

In this section we begin the more practical work of developing the skills of argumentation, delivery, and flowing. Without a doubt, persuasive arguments win debates. This refers to the logic and reasoning that the debater uses.

Accordingly, the Greek philosopher Aristotle is reported to have made the statement:

"What you say is more important than how you say it".
On the contrary, the Greek orator Demosthenes is reported to have made the following statement:

"It's not what you say, it's how you say it".

Regardless of whether one is inclined to agree with Aristotle or Demosthenes, one thing is clear: Debaters need to be able to construct a convincing argument, deliver that argument in front of a live audience, and follow the arguments the opposing team is using.

This means making notes of what is being said during the debate. Let's look closer at these three topics.

**

# CHAPTER 7:

# ARGUMENTATION

Before making our argument, it is a good idea to review how a debate is judged. There are three basic areas to consider: Content, Organisation, and Delivery.

Content can be understood as the amount of understanding of, and support for, the topic. Hence, content is the **Argument** itself. Organisation is the planning and preparation of the argument.

Thus, organisation includes the **Reasons** and the **Evidence** used to support your position. As a result, we now have the basic argument model, A-R-E (adapted from Snider 2008, p. 122):

**A** - Argument

**R** – Reason

**E** – Evidence

Example: Motion: THB marijuana should be legalised.

**Argument**: Marijuana is not more harmful than tobacco or alcohol.

**Reason**(s): *Research shows* that nicotine is far more addictive than marijuana.

**Evidence**: *For example*, in an editorial in the **Times (UK), August 6, 2001**, Dr. Colin Blakemore, **Chair, Department of Physiology**, from Oxford University,wrote: "Unlike for nicotine, alcohol and hard drugs, there is **no clearly defined withdrawal syndrome**, the **hallmark of true addiction**, when [marijuana] use is stopped."

**L** – Link: **This means** substances **more harmful** than marijuana are legal while marijuana is not. **Therefore**, to remedy this **injustice**, marijuana should be legalised.

\*\*

# CHAPTER 8:

# DELIVERY

Delivery (style) is how the debater speaks. It includes both verbal and nonverbal elements:

| Verbal | Nonverbal |
|---|---|
| Pronunciation, tone, volume, speed, pitch, emotions, i.e. sarcasm, indignation, pity, etc. | Eye contact, gestures, facial expressions, posture, movement, personality, attitude. |

There are five things speakers need to consider in their delivery:

**A** – Audibility: Speakers need to be heard by everyone.

**E** – Engagement: Getting and keeping the audience attention.
**C** – Conviction: Show true concern for the topic.

**A** – Authority: You know what you are talking about.

**L** – Likability: Be nice, play fair. Smile, this is not a war.

**Audibility** is essential for the judges, your opponents, and the members of the audience. If there is a microphone, practice before the debate so you will know how to use it properly. If there is no microphone, practice "hitting targets", that is, speaking from your diaphragm so that you can be comfortably heard at various locations, front to back, in the room.

**Engagement** means using a variety of means to maintain the attention of the audience. Vary the volume of your voice, the rate of speech, the tone, even the emotion you show, in order to keep your audience from dozing off or wandering off in a daydream while you are speaking. Make your gestures appear natural, coordinating your movements and facial expressions to be coherent with what you are saying. Making eye contact with the audience is a good way to engage with your audience.

**Conviction** means personal involvement with what you are talking about. If you are not convinced in the rightness of your message, then why should the audience believe you either? Study the topic from a number of angles. Talk to people who have been affected by the issue you are considering. Ask yourself a personal question: "Why should I care about this topic?" When you know the answer, you will be able to speak with conviction.

**Authority** means knowing your facts, figures, supporting evidence, and any examples thoroughly. This means you have analysed not only the arguments in favour of your position but also the arguments in contra. You are prepared for anything.

This requires research for a speech prepared in advance. For an impromptu debate speech, with only 15 minutes advance notice, you will find yourself benefitting from a regular program of reading an informative newspaper or magazine daily. Instead of reading the sports section only, begin to read daily on politics, the economy, business, and current events. This will give you a basic foundation in the issues that are important in the world we live in today.

**Likability**, the most difficult element of delivery, begins the moment you enter the debate venue. You are being watched by your opponents and your judges. Your opponents want to "size you up", get a feel for your level of maturity, your level of self – confidence, the level of friendship and trust that exists between you, your teammates, and your coach.

The judges are trying to "get a feel" for what they can expect from you as a speaker. They notice how you are dressed, the way you wear your clothes, the expression of confidence, nervousness or anxiety that may be evident in your face or in your body language.

A word of advice: "Look, think, and act like a winner at all times". This means all times, even when you have doubts. Remember, the other team is going through the same exact situation as you are.

Finally, always show respect and courtesy for your opponents. You will be tempted to call them names: naive – stupid – dumb. **RESIST** the impulse to do so. It is the easiest way to lose the respect of the judges and the audience. Once you show that you are not a true gentleman or lady, a positive connection with the judges or audience will be lost forever.

Show humility in victory. You won because you were lucky. Show grace in defeat. Congratulate your opponents with a firm handshake. You did your best. Today you didn't win, but there will be another day – today simply wasn't your day – but your day is coming.

**

# CHAPTER 9:

# FLOWING

Flowing means taking notes. Yes, you are actually supposed to listen to what your opponents are saying. Since you can't remember everything they say, you need to write down their arguments, reasons, evidence, and links (AREL). This will help you to rebut the arguments against your position. You must always rebut your opponents arguments at the first opportunity.

Think of it like this: If you were in a boxing match and you got hit in the first round, would you wait until the fourth and final round before you tried to hit your opponent back with a harder blow? Of course not, right? Then why would you do something in a verbal battle that you would not do in a physical battle? You must clash with your opponents' ideas whenever and wherever they present you with an opportunity. Clash is what a debate is all about. Clash impresses judges because it shows your ability to think on your feet.

Again, do not get in the habit of waiting until the final summary speech to do your rebuttal. By that time, most judges will already have made up their minds about the point in question. This means that when you are not speaking, you are taking notes, attentively listening to the other team. You should not make your speech and sit down – saying to yourself – "I gave my speech" – "I'm finished for the day". No-no-no!

No, you still have a responsibility to your teammates to use your intellectual gifts for the benefit of your team. You take notes down on what is being said, passing on any ideas you may have about an argument that you hear – it could be something your teammates didn't understand, didn't hear, or simply didn't think it was important. Be a team player, do everything in your power to help your team win.

So, how do you "flow"? It's hard to write down what people are saying. They talk fast, they don't pronounce their words clearly, they mumble and stumble – and I'm supposed to be taking notes, yeah right. There has gotta be an easy way to do this, isn't there?

Answer: No, there is no easy way to flow a debate. You gotta practice an awful lot.

**How to Flow**

Take notes in your English classes.
Take notes in your Math classes.
Take notes in your Science classes.
Take notes in your History classes.
Take notes in your Biology classes.
Take notes when you are watching the news.
Take notes when you are watching a movie.
Take notes when someone is practicing a speech.
Take notes when someone is singing a song.

Take notes when your debate Coach makes a speech.

Develop your own shorthand system. Try writing words without vowels. Use the **A-R-E** model to write down only the important information. Omit the little words.

## Flow Activity

Divide your paper into four columns. Label each column with the name of the speaker:

| 1st Proposition | 1st Opposition | 2nd Proposition | 2nd Opposition |
|---|---|---|---|
|  |  |  |  |

Repeat the same thing on another sheet of paper:

| 3rd Proposition | 3rd Opposition | 4th Proposition: | 4th Opposition: |
|---|---|---|---|
|  |  |  |  |

## Debate Practice Activities:

1. Argumentation Drill: **The Why Game**

Students form a circle. Each student in turn enters the circle and makes the statement: "I believe we should ban (or legalise) something." The other students respond, "Why?" The student in the circle answers, "Because..." This continues until the student is unable to continue, then another student enters the circle and the drill begins all over again.

For example:
A: I believe we should legalise marijuana.
All Students: Why?
A: Because it's not addictive.
All Students: Why?
A: Because _____
All Students: Why?
A: Because _____

2. Pronunciation Drill: **Pencil Poetry**.

Students place a pencil in their mouth (sideways). A poem must be read – clearly. Sounds simple enough, right?

The reality is that many students will sound horrible at first, but with a little practice, they will soon sound better than they do when they don't have a pencil sideways in their mouth! When this happens, it's because of the muscular exertion to enunciate clearly.

| "Invictus" by William Ernest Henley | |
|---|---|
| **Verse 1** | **Verse 2** |
| Out of the night that covers me, | In the fell clutch of circumstance, |
| Black as the pit from pole to pole, | I have not winced, nor cried aloud, |
| | Under the bludgeonings of chance, |
| I thank whatever Gods may be, | My head is bloody, but |
| For my unconquerable soul. | unbowed. |
| **Verse 3** | **Verse 4** |
| Beyond this place of wrath and tears, | It matters not how strait the gate, |
| Looms but the horror of the shade, | How charged with punishments the scroll, |
| Yet, the menace of the years, | I am the Master of my Fate, |
| Finds, and shall find me, unafraid. | I am the Captain of my Soul. |

3. Critical Thinking Drill: **Defending the Indefensible**

Students are seated. One by one a student is given an indefensible statement to defend.

Example: All people should ride a zebra to work.
Defense: Zebras don't pollute the air.

4. Delivery Drill: **Ma Ma Moo**

Students are seated. One by one a student comes to the front of the room, is given an emotion, (happy , sad, etc) which can only be represented by saying, "ma ma moo".

5. Argumentation Drill: **Balloon Debate**

Famous people, in a sinking balloon, can only save themselves by making an argument to throw someone out while the rest of the people remain in the ballon. Students vote after each round, eliminating one speaker per round, until only one speaker remains, "alive".

Example: Mother Teresa, Beyonce, Bill Gates, Hillary Clinton, The Pope, Pamela Anderson, Marcelo Bielsa, Chupete Suazo, Madonna, Chaleco Lopez, Tiger Woods, etc.

6. Audience Engagement Drill: **Look Me in The Eye**

Students are standing in a circle. An impromptu topic is given to a student. The student enters the circle and begins to speak. While speaking, the student walks slowly but naturally around the circle, briefly and naturally **looking each student in the eyes**. The student speaks extemporaneously on the topic given (inventing the speech).

7. Argument Drill: **If I Ruled The World**

Students are standing. Students introduce themselves in the following way:

"Good morning. My name is Tom. I'm from Santiago and if I ruled the world I would make everybody wear blue shoes **because** I think they are cool."

"Good afternoon. My name is Gaby. I'm from Concepción and if I ruled the world I would make all world leaders be women **because** women are smarter than men.

8. Rebuttal Drill: **A Moral Dilemma**

Students are standing facing each other in two lines. A moral dilemma is presented, for example: "You find a wallet with a million Chilean pesos in it but it has **no identifying information**. One side (**proposition**) must give reasons (15 to 20 seconds) why they would **give the wallet to the police**. The other side (**opposition**) must give **rebuttal** (15 to 20 seconds) to the argument given and give reasons why they would **keep the money**.

$1^{st}$ Prop Speaker: I believe you should turn it in to the police because the person who lost it will go to the police station and ask for it.

$1^{st}$ Opp Speaker: The problem with giving it to the police is that there is no identifying information and therefore the money will go to the government. And I don't think the government needs it more than I do.

$2^{nd}$ Prop Speaker: But the person who lost the wallet can identify it.

$2^{nd}$ Opp Speaker: He won't be able to because I will keep the money.

$3^{rd}$ Prop Speaker: But is it right for you to keep money which isn't yours?

$3^{rd}$ Opp Speaker: Yes, it is – Finders Keepers, Losers Weepers.

9. Delivery Drill: **Count Me A Joke**

Each student comes to the front.and **tells a joke**. Students are only allowed to use numbers, counting from 1 to 20. For students who aren't funny, they may "**Count A Story**" again, only using numbers, from 1 to 20. Students need to use gestures, varied speed, varied volume, movement, varied pitch and tone, facial expressions, etc.

10. Rebuttal Drill: **Three Things Wrong**

The coach makes a one minute speech. Students, in turn, give a 15 to 30 second rebuttal: "My opponents say_____, but there are **three things wrong** with it. First, _____ . Second, _____ . Thirdly, _____ .

\*\*

# PART FOUR:

# STRATEGY

Strategy is probably understood narrowly by most debaters. "How am I going to make my speech? What am I going to talk about?" These are the questions that come to mind when a debater begins to think about strategy.

Yet strategy begins with research, out of which the **team line** and the **team split** emerge, eventually resulting in victory or defeat. For these reasons, strategy must be broadly viewed.

Therefore, we begin this final section not by talking about the roles of the individual speakers, but with research.

**

# CHAPTER 10:

# RESEARCH

Research is something that debaters should do every day, in a general sense. Specific research on a given debate topic should begin by consulting a topic synthesis, and in-depth research should begin by talking with the people who are intimately connected with the topic. These three areas, daily research, synthesis research, and human research, form a **Research Pyramid**, with all elements being equally important.

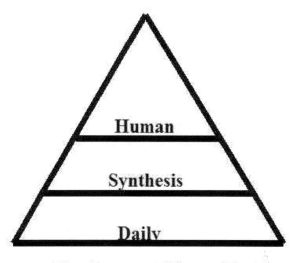

**The Research Pyramid**

**Daily** research forms the base of the pyramid, serving as the foundation upon which the other two research elements are built. Daily research requires debaters to be curious, inquisitive, critically minded individuals who enjoy being informed about the world they live in. This means reading, reading, reading, and more reading. Newspapers and magazines that include both local and national news should be read.

Over time, debaters **build up** a knowledge of current events, different perspectives and a general storehouse of information that can be called upon in a debate. Magazines, like Newsweek, the Economist, and the Wall Street Journal are highly recommendable. Newspapers like El Mercurio, Las Ultimas Noticias, El Segundo, and La Nación, should be read, paying particular attention to the editorials and letters to the editor. It goes without saying that a wide variety of topics should be read. With all of these newspapers freely available on-line, cost is not an issue.

Television and radio form another important avenue of being informed about the events of our world. Watching the evening news, on a variety of TV stations, is recommendable. The investment in time will result in an appreciable increase in knowledge about how the events of our time are represented in the news.

It will demonstrate what issues are continuously present, what issues are usually present, and what issues are rarely present. This knowledge will certainly be beneficial to a debater when preparing an impromptu debate speech, or in an extemporaneous speaking situation where one must rely on personal knowledge. This brings us to **synthesis**, our second level in the research pyramid.

**Synthesis** is an equal component of the research pyramid. Synthesis means taking advantage of information on a topic that has already been summarised, by someone else. An example of this would be "Cliff's Notes", which specialise in summaries about an infinite number of topics. Also, a specific source of debate information is provided by various debate organisations.

What is important, however, is not the summary so much, as the understanding that a summary or synthesis about a topic is *not* the end point of research. Debaters who prepare for a debate by only referring to a summary will surely find themselves limited. The limitations of your knowledge will be defined by the quality of the source consulted. In a close debate, this could make the difference between winning and losing.

Therefore, make it a habit not to refer only to a synthesis as the basis for preparing your speech. The summary should give you ideas about further research to undertake. In this way, you can triangulate, or gather together a number of sources, that inform your views that you then present in your argumentation. This must be integrated with **human research**, our third element in the research triangle.

**Human research** means talking to <u>**people**</u>. Debate is about the real world, so it follows that much is to be learned by talking to <u>real people</u> affected by <u>real events</u>. This human dimension should prove enlightening, especially when one explores both sides of an issue. A better understanding of a problem is gained by listening to how people are affected, both positively and negatively, about the events of the world.

To do **human research**, the debater is well advised to interview family members and friends as well as professionals in the community. In this way, debaters will most likely discover their own personal stake in the issue. This in turn leads to conviction and authority, which is the source of many an impassioned debate speech. Without a doubt, when you are personally and internally convinced of the rightness and righteousness of the position you are speaking for, your audience and the judges will also be convinced.

\*\*

# CHAPTER 11:

# TEAM SPLIT

Consider the following opening speech by the First Proposition speaker. The motion is, **THB voting should be compulsory**.

First Proposition Speaker's Speech

**"Good evening, ladies and gentlemen of the jury, members of the audience, and opposition team.** My name is **Juan Perés** and **I represent Colegio El Poeta**. The members of my team are **María Gonzalez, Pedro Tapia**, and **José Cienfuegos**.

**Our motion today is**, "This House Believes voting should be compulsory". President Abraham Lincoln, in his Gettysburg Address, said, "...government of the people, by the people, for the people – shall not perish from this Earth". Ladies and gentlemen, history agrees with Abraham Lincoln.

**My team** also agrees with Abraham Lincoln. Today, **we will prove** that government    needs the participation of the people, *even if* it requires **compulsory voting**.

**3.** For our **team strategy**, *I will talk about* why Abraham Lincoln had to disregard civil rights and fight a civil war to preserve democracy. Then *Maria will talk about* how democracy is **harmed** when the people do not vote. Pedro *will talk about* how democracy **benefits** from compulsory voting. José will **summarize** our **main points** and tell you **why my team should win this debate**.

**4.** *Before we begin*, it is important to **define** the term, "compulsory". **According to** the 2010 Cambridge Learner's Dictionary, "compulsory" is an adjective that means, "something that you must do because of a rule or law".

**5.** **I turn now to my first argument**, democracy must be preserved, *even if* it requires **compulsory voting**. Abraham Lincoln proved that, **I quote**, *"A house divided against itself can not stand"*. **We** can all agree with Lincoln when he said, "Half slave and half free, no democracy can exist".

**6.** When *the people* of a country **do not vote**, for whatever reason, then that country is a **house divided against itself**. This means, in one *house*, the **people** who vote are **free**. In the other *house*, the **people** who do **not** vote have become **slaves** to the arbitrary desires of the people who vote. **A house divided against itself can not stand.**

**7.** Ladies and gentlemen, **the opposition team is going to tell you** we have a right **not to vote** – even if it requires a Civil War to secure the right, **not** to vote. **They are wrong** because of all the pain and suffering that war brings. **They are wrong because of all** the death and destruction that war brings. **They are wrong because** war is immoral and inhumane. For example, according to historical records, 600,000 men died in the United States Civil War, 2% of the population of the entire United States.

**8. However**, in contrast to the opposition team, **my team** has a **peaceful** *solution*. **We believe compulsory voting will preserve**

**government of the people, by the people, for the people.** Thank you very much." \*\*\* End of Speech

Discussion:

In this model speech, we find all of the elements of an excellent First Speech. Overall team strategy is clearly evident and directly referred to. This prepares the judges for what they will be hearing, making the arguments in the debate easier to recognise, especially for an inexperienced judge or a celebrity who is judging. Let's go through the speech paragraph by paragraph.

In paragraph 1, the purpose is clear. First, the speaker greets everyone present. Then the speaker introduces himself and his teammates.

In paragraph 2, the debate topic (the motion) is announced. Additionally, a brief quotation is given that is relevant to the motion. This is a matter of style – it is not required. Hence, it could be omitted. Finally, a clear statement of what the proposition speaker's team will prove in the debate is given. In the opposition speech, the same thing should be done.

In paragraph 3, the team strategy is announced. We can see that it is logically constructed and cohesive. The first speaker will connect to the quotation that was used, the second speaker will address **harms**, the third speaker will address **benefits**, and the final speaker will **summarise** and make a case for why his team has **won** the debate.

How the overall team arguments are divided among the speakers is known as the **team split**. As we can see, it allows the judges to anticipate the speeches in advance, and more importantly, lets the judges know that this is a team that is working together. Often, poor debaters will develop their speeches in isolation, not having a clue about what their teammates will be talking about, nor how each speech makes a **unified argument** overall.

In paragraph 4, the key term for the debate is defined. This is necessary for both teams to do, even when the terms appear clear. Do not omit defining terms. It tells the audience and judges how you understand the key words in the debate.

In paragraph 5, the speaker uses a **signal phrase**, "I turn now to my first argument". This makes it clear to the judges what the speaker is going to talk about. This makes it easier for the judge to take notes – to <u>flow</u> the debate. This ensures the speaker that key points won't be missed. Also, notice the use of the pronoun *we*, it's inclusive and engages the audience.

In paragraph 6, the speaker makes an analogy. The purpose is to compare one thing to a similar thing to argue that they both share similar principles. It follows that they both should be regarded in the same way, with the same value attached to each. Argument by analogy is not sufficient alone but its use can help to make the team's position stronger.

In paragraph 7, the speaker, First Proposition, is anticipating the argument of the First Opposition speaker. First Proposition has already made his argument, and is now offering rebuttal to what **will most likely, probably** be said by the opposing team. First Proposition speaker is the only speaker who does not follow another speaker from the opposition team, which is a disadvantage. Therefore, First Proposition resorts to this strategy of rebutting an anticipated overall argument in order to neutralise the opposition advantage.

In paragraph 8, the speaker draws a contrast in order to clearly differentiate his team from the opposition team. This contrast is designed to create a favorable comparison for the Proposition team. The final sentence is the **team line**. *Every speaker* on the Proposition team <u>will finish their speech</u> by saying that *same phrase*, clearly indicating teamwork, strategy, continuity and clarity of purpose throughout the debate: **<u>We believe compulsory voting will preserve government of the people, by the people, for the people.</u>**

\*\*

# CHAPTER 12:

# VICTORY & DEFEAT

In debate, there are literally, no "losers". Everyone is a "winner". For this reason alone, I encourage teachers to incorporate debate into their classrooms. It doesn't matter whether you debate in a classroom or in a competition, every participant has competed primarily with themselves, challenged themselves to reach the limits of their potential, and in so doing, enriched their lives profoundly.

The judges' decision, in your team's favor or against it, can not reduce your personal satisfaction in having done your best: before, during, and after the competition. Having done your best, you are a winner. That is what debating is all about, in the final analysis: doing your best.

According to John Wooden, the most successful basketball coach in history, winning nine national championships at the University of Californa at Los Angeles (UCLA):

**"Success is peace of mind that is a direct result of self-satisfaction in knowing you made the effort to become the best that you are capable of becoming".**

**Exercise:**

**Exercise:  Strategy Evaluation: Chilean MINEDUC Debate**
The purpose of this exercise is to evaluate the speeches from the 2008 National Final Debate Competition.  The two teams participating are Liceo Amanda Labarca from Santiago, Región Metropolitana (Proposition  Team) and Colegio Santa Emilia from Antofagasta, Segunda Región (Opposition Team).

The **twenty-one** (21) judges for the debate are:

Mr. Alex Fernandez (COBA),
Mr. Norbert Kalisch (Ambassador of Canada),
Mr. Abdullah Zain (Ambassador of Malaysia),
Ms. Jöelle Uzarski (Regional English Language Officer – United States Embassy)
Davina Potts (Education, Training, and Science Officer – Australian Training & Education International),
Daniella Truco (Educational Coordinator – United Nations),
Charles Couteau (BBC Journalist),
Anna Lorensen (Director of NAFCO from Sweden),
Constanza Proto (Academic Program Manager from Microsoft Chile),
Cecilia Gomez (Cambridge University Press),
Juan Carlos Corea (Instituto Chileno-Norteamericano de Cultura),
Carmen Figueroa (El Mercurio),
Carmen Coyunam (International Consultant),
Pedro Pfeiffer (Director – Chilean British University),
Javier Cox (Director for Chile Transporte),
Gilbert Leiva (Executive Director – International Holding),
Alejandro Maignon (United Nations Officer),
Professor Gregory Elacqua (Universidad Adolfo Ibañez ),
Mateo Budnevich (President of AMCHAM),
Hernán Ibañez (Corporación Aprender), and
Rodrigo Fábrega (Director – English Opens Doors Program).
Last but not least: Debate Chairperson -
The Honourable Mónica Jimenez de la Jara,
(Chilean Minister of Education).

\*\*\*

The Motion is:
**THBT the internet has a positive influence on society.**

1<sup>st</sup> Proposition Speaker: Maria José Court  (3 minutes)
(Maria delivers her speech **standing behind the podium**, with a microphone)

"**Good morning** audience and judges. My name is Maria José Court and I represent Amanda Labarca Public School. We believe that the internet is a positive influence on society, which is what the <u>thesis</u> says. **But before we begin**, we must <u>define some key terms</u>. **First**, the internet, which is a decentralised global network based on the interrelation between millions of computers with shared information. The **second and most important term** in the <u>thesis</u>, is the word, **positive**, since the debate is based on it. Eh, since **according to the Dictionary of the Real Academia Española**, it means something that is: "useful and practical". **That is what we have to prove today**, since any argument based on the **moral** content of the internet, is **strictly, completely, straying from the thesis**. Since the important thing here is the definition of "useful", which means effective, something that helps you do or achieve a certain thing. And "practical", which means "to provide effective solutions to problems". Here we can find the recurrent use of the word, "effective", which means to produce the desired effect. <u>What is the internet desired effect?</u> It was created in the

44

United States for military purposes to facilitate inter-communication. It was so effective that it spread throughout the world, not just as a means of communications, but also to share information. <u>So, what does this tell us?</u> That it was so successful, that not only did it accomplish its initial desired effect, but it surpassed it by far. **So**, the **purpose** of this debate is to prove that the internet **fulfills** its purpose. <u>For if it is useful and practical to the user, it is therefore positive</u>. **The opposition team may say** that we are basing ourself in a "**fallacy of hasty generalization**", which consists on attribute a characteristic of a particular case to a whole. Since the <u>thesis</u> states that the **entire** internet has a positive influence on society. **But**, be careful, because if the **generalization** is correct, then the statement is not a fallacy. **So**, there is no fallacy present in our argumentation, since "positive" means something that is useful and practical, a quality that is present in **all of the internet**, and "<u>**we cannot deny this**</u>", since it is a tool that has influenced society in a positive way by providing an **almost unlimited source** of information – **an efficient method of communication**. Then, **the information shared is irrelevant in this debate** since all that matters here is if the tool is useful in its purpose. So, finally, from all of **this,** everyone should understand that "positive" is not the same as morally good. Thank You.

*** *End of 1^st Proposition Speech*
1^st Opposition Speaker:  Rebecca Rodriguez    (3 minutes)
(Rebecca delivers her speech with a **microphone in her hand, freely moving on stage**)

"**Good afternoon**, Chairperson, Timekeeper, **adjudicators**, Ladies and Gentlemen of the audience, and Members of the Proposition.  My name is Rebecca, and I'm the first opposition speaker for this debate.  We, are representing Colegio Santa Emilia from the  Antofagasta Region, and this is my team: second speaker, Fernando; third speaker, Sebastián; and our fourth and final speaker, Nolvia.  We, **are going to be proving to you**, how the internet **is not** a positive influence on society, but, in fact, a **negative** one.  The internet is an "**am-aaa-zing**" technology.  And when people have used it for communication purposes, it should have positive influences on society, right?  **Wrong**.  The internet actually **harms participation in community life and social relationships**.  **Numerous studies have documented** what is commonly referred to as, "the internet paradox".  A **prior** study showed that the greater use of the internet was <u>significantly</u> associated with <u>decreased</u> communication within the family, <u>decreased</u> social local networks, <u>loneliness</u> and depression. A **Stanford University study showed** that this loss of social contact was noticeable, which is <u>2 to 5 internet hours per week</u>. And it rises <u>substantially</u> for those spending more than 10 hours per week, **contradicting the proposition team**, <u>who claim that the internet increases social content with communication.</u> An additional brain and psychological study showed that the average person uses the internet for 19 hours per week, making it very challenging to maintain a healthy social life. Now, this number is ever increasing. And as such, people are developing serious addiction to various parts of the internet.

Although, is internet addiction even that common? Actually, "Yes". The Stanford University study also showed that 1 out of 8 Americans, "**suffer from internet addiction**", which can range from compulsive surfing, to cyber-sex and porn addiction.

But, what are the <u>consequences</u> of internet addiction? Well, the Center for Internet Addiction Recovery tells us that children who have internet addictions are more likely to <u>suffer</u> from depression, to develop physical illnesses, and to experience social and academic problems at school. On-line gambling, and E-bay addicts, lose excessive amounts of money, and neglect job-related duties, and important relationships. There is a **tragic example** from South Korea, where a four-month-old baby **died**, because she was left alone while her parents played on-line games on Internet Cafe. The <u>Internet</u> has brought about a world where you can order anything you want on-line. **But you don't even know your neighbors**. Where children and parents spend all evening talking to distant strangers, <u>rather than each other</u>! **This, is not a positive influence on society.** Thank You.

*** *End of 1ˢᵗ Opposition Speech*

**Exercise:**

**Ticking the Boxes**

Speech Analysis:

Using the chart below, analyse the speech by writing "Yes" or "No", for each category/ aspect of the speech.

Feel free to add any comments you feel necessary.

After you have finished, watch the video of the debate:

http://video.google.es/videoplay?docid=321090705448405420#

How did watching the delivery of the speech change your analysis of the speech?

| Evaluation / Analysis of 1<sup>st</sup> Speeches: | | |
|---|---|---|
| **Category** | **Amanda Labarca** | **Santa Emilia** |
| | | |
| **Introduction** | | |
| Announce Motion | | |
| Team Strategy | | |
| Team Split | | |
| "We will prove" | | |
| Define key terms | | |
| **Signal Phrase** | | |
| Pronoun We/Us | | |
| Argumentation (**AREL**) | | |
| Rebuttal "**wrong**" | | |
| Contrast: Differentiation | | |
| **Team Line** | | |
| **A**udibility | | |
| **E**ngagement | | |
| **C**onviction | | |
| **A**uthority | | |
| **L**ikability | | |
| FairPlay (Squirrel) | | |
| Time Used (3 minutes) | | |
| **Conclusion** | | |
| Comments Remarks | | |

2nd Proposition Speaker: Maria Betanía Bunster  (3 minutes)
(Maria delivers her speech **standing behind the podium**, with a microphone)

"Good morning.  My name is María Betanía Bunster and I'm representing Amanda Labarca Public School.  The opposition team has only mentioned the morally bad content of the internet.  **Is this a topic of the debate**?  Is the word – moral – or good influence – present in the **thesis**?  No.  This unfortunately shows that you haven't understood the **thesis**.   Since we've established that the topic of this debate is, "Is the internet completely positive?"  We have debated strictly on the thesis.  And every word used on it.  **Why?**  According to the debating manual provided by the Ministry of Education, "The arguments presented on a debate must not stray from the thesis".  Since if they do, the team won't be debating properly.

Now, to prove that the internet is in fact positive, let's talk about life **before** and **after** this tool.  Before we had access to the internet, life was more complex and slower than it is now.  There were means of communication available, but they were slower and not as efficient.   The telephone was the quickest way to communicate, but the international affairs were unaffordable.

Letters, depending on the destination, could take weeks, or even months to get there. Research was long and tedious. Library trips, to consult giant encyclopedias, were made often, and valuable time was wasted trying to find the appropriate information.

In contrast to this situation, we find ourselves with our reality. In which speed, a better management of the available resources, and the easy access to information, which are the common scenario. The response of this is the internet. (Voice cracking) One of the most used applications today is email. A means that allows for an almost instant communication between millions of people. **According to** the **BBBA Foundation**, an **84%** of the Spanish population uses email. And **97%** use search engines.

But is this tool actually positive? Meaning, useful or practical to the user? <u>Like the first speaker said</u>, "When something is useful it means, "that it helps you to achieve something".

But when is the internet useful? Think about it. You're all students.What do you do when you need to do research for your homework? If you're preparing for a debate, "What is the <u>main</u> source of information that you would go to?" The answer is only one. You use the internet."

So, we have established that this tool helps you to achieve many goals. That include communicating, researching, and saving valuable time. Even more, it has been so efficient that it has begun to replace other means of communication. Therefore, we can say that the internet is in fact, positive, because it helps you do and achieve what you want. Thank You.

*** *End of 2<sup>nd</sup> Proposition Speech*

2<sup>nd</sup> Opposition Speaker: Fernando Muñoz   (3 minutes)
(Fernando delivers his speech with a **microphone in his hand, freely moving on stage**)

"Good afternoon, Ladies and Gentlemen.   My name is Fernando Muñoz, and I am the second opposition speaker for this debate. **I'm going to be talking about** how the dangers of anonymous internet have **devastating consequences** on society.

**You said** that children can use internet for educational purposes. And, Yes, children have embraced the internet as they go on-line to learn, play, and even communicate with their friends. But actually, the internet is an almost perfect medium for offenders, seeking children for sex. It provides privacy, anonymity, and a virtually unlimited pool of unsupervised children and teenagers whom are susceptible to manipulation. These offenders no longer need to lurk in parks and malls.

Instead, they stalk vulnerable kids from chatroom to chatroom. There is **phenomenal** growth in social networking sites, such as Facebook, Facebook, or MySpace. And young people, have been putting personal information, including countless photos, on their profiles. This information, makes it easily traceable to online predators, of which the UK police, claim to be over 50 thousand, **prowling** the internet, at **any – given – time**. Research, conducted by the National Center For Missing and Exploited Children, disclosed during the past year, 1 in 5 children, **1-in-5**, received sexual advances, over the internet.

**Furthermore**, the internet provides a voice for <u>pedophiles</u>, that in the past, operated alone and without the luxury, of communicating with other like-minded individuals. Now, they share <u>pictures</u>, <u>videos</u>, and <u>stories</u>, of their <u>perverse</u> - <u>child</u> - <u>conquests</u>. Of course, children and teens aren't just **vulnerable** to attacks from strangers, but also, from other children, and teens.

<u>**Deaths**</u>, come in the form of cyber-bullying. And now to do supplements live, in person. Bullying. <u>Torment, does not stop when the bell rings</u>. Bullies can now **threaten, harrass, humiliate**, [*** -"humiliate" - spoken with a higher tone - forcefully]and **embarrass** your classmates, **24 hours a day – 7 days a week**.

Cyber-bullying has <u>**deadly**</u> consequences. Two kids from the United States committed **<u>suicide</u>** after being deceived and ridiculed by false internet attacks, perpetrated by their abusive peers. The internet provides <u>cyber-bullies</u> and <u>sexual predators</u>, with the <u>anonymity</u> to <u>abuse children</u>, and <u>exploit children</u>, at levels **not previously possible** in our society. Thank You.

*\*\*\*End of 2<sup>nd</sup> Opposition Speech*

3rd Proposition Speaker: Catalina Araneda  (3 minutes)
(Catalina delivers her speech **standing behind the podium**, with a microphone)

"First of all, I would like to say that the first and second speaker of the opposition team keeps talking about the content on the internet. But, they haven't realised that by doing that, they are supporting us <u>because</u> that shows that the internet provides information to anyone. It doesn't matter if the content is morally good or morally bad, <u>because</u> it's still **being useful and practical**.

Good morning. My name is Catalina Araneda and I represent Amanda Labarca Public School. Every tool can be used in many ways. For good or bad intentions but, regardless of that, the tool remains the same. It does not lose the capacity to perform the function for which it was created. When this tool is used inappropriately it doesn't mean that it stops being positive. Furthermore, this inappropriate use, it only increase the utility of the tool, since it adds a new ability to the already existing.

People confuse what's morally good and what's positive because they try to attribute negative qualities to the net. But, there's no argument that can take away this tool's quality to be useful and practical – therefore positive. Because it helps to achieve our purpose. If we focus on the information shared by the users, it could be morally bad, like websites that promote prostitution, pedophilia, theft of confidential information, etc.

But on the other hand, we can find websites that promote ideas considered good, such as environmentalism, fraternity, religion, democracy, etc. However, all of this is irrelevant for this debate. Why? Because according to the thesis, the important thing here, is to prove, if the internet is a positive influence on society. Which, according to the definition of positive, **we know is true**.

So, let me give you an example to let this situation even more clear. If I want to grow marijuana, the internet must provide me the information to do so. **Why**? This is morally good? Of course it's not, but is it **positive**? <u>**Yes, it is**</u>. **Because** it helps me to achieve my purpose.

In the same way, if I want to publish instructions on how to perform First Aid, the internet should give me the possibility to do so. Seeing, as like before, if it doesn't, then it's no longer usefel or practical. So, **how can you deny the fact** that the internet is a positive influence on society?

When we have proved in all ways, that this tool is effective in all of its appliations? Well, like the first speaker said, "Talk about the internet's faults, because the child is going to be addicted to it, but – Is the internet the fault of this? **No.** Of course not. Thank you.

***End of Third Proposition Speech*

3rd Opposition Speaker: Sebastián Escobedo   (3 minutes)
(Sebastián delivers his speech with a **microphone in his hand, freely moving on stage**)

"Good afternoon everyone. <u>You have claimed, that we don't understand the thesis</u>. Yet, **we believe**, that it's actually **you** who have <u>forgotten **half** of the thesis</u>. **Yes, the internet is positive** in <u>that it's useful and practical</u>, **however**, in doing so, it's **undeniably** having a **negative influence** on society. **For example**, <u>I'm going to explain</u> to you how the internet provides new opportunities, for criminals to **terrorise** and **deprive** society.

But how does the internet result in crime? Well, the traditional barriers for criminals have been **obliterated** by digital technologies. **In the past**, the culprit had to be physically present to commit a crime. <u>**Now**</u>, cyber-crimes can be committed from anywhere in the world. And as the internet becomes more sophisticated, so do the crimes.

Additionally, an article in the **British Journal of Criminology**, claims that as computer systems are acting as a buffer, between the offenders, and the victims, people are more likely to engage in criminal behaviour on-line, than they would in the physical world. The cost of cyber crume is high, and it's still growing!

If we look at all the internet **crimes in 2006** alone, we see that the total loss is 198 Million dollars. With an average loss of 724 (dollars) per complaint.

The internet is also being used by groups committed to **terrorising** our society. Today, all terrorist groups have established their presence on the internet. And there are many different ways in which contemporary terrorists can use the internet. Ranging from psychological warfare and propoganda, to fund-raising and even recruitment. They do not only use it to learn how to build bombs, no, but to plan and coordinate specific attacks. An example of this, is that Al Qaeda operatives rely **heavily** on the internet to plan and coordinate the 2001, September 11 attacks in New York. Thousands of encrypted messages were found in a populated area of a website from an arrested Al Qaeda terrorist, who reportedly, masterminded the attacks.

Internet crime results in **Hundreds of Millions of dollars of losses, facilitatates terrorist activities,** and with the advancements in hacking techniques, **the internet has effectively brought criminals, into-every-home.** Thank You.

\*\*\*End of 3<sup>rd</sup> Opposition Speech

4<sup>th</sup> Proposition Speaker: Camila Rossel  (3 minutes – Summary Speech)
(Camila delivers her speech **standing behind the podium**, with a microphone)

"Good afternoon, audience, judges. My name is Camila Rossel, and I represent Amanda Labarca Public School. First of all, **you talked about**, the second speaker talked about the dangers of children while they are on the internet. Well, I'm sorry. Have you heard of responsible parenting? Or parental controlled software? This is the solution. You talked about bullying on the internet. Who are the people? The people does the bullying, not the internet.

Now, we are not here to discuss if the information present on the internet is morally good or not. **What we are here to discuss is if the internet has been and is a positive influence on society**. Taking into account all the arguments that we have given you, there is **absolutely no doubt** that the internet is a useful and practical tool. **Therefore**, according to the definitions provided by the RAE, among other dictionaries, we can be sure that this tool is in fact, **positive**.

All of the arguments of the opposition **completely strayed from the thesis**, since, what we are talking about here, is the internet, and its influence, **thus**, we need to focus on its functions.

These are: providing an efficient method of communication, and a way for people to share information. Both of these are performed by the internet in an excellent manner. The content of this information is **irrelevant**, **since**, it doesn't affect this tool's functions. Furthermore, the vast information contained by the internet, the better its performance.

Now, it is true that the internet can influence our lives in many different ways. But we are the ones in charge of deciding **how** it will affect them. **We make our own decisions, don't we?** The net can **not** affect us **negatively**. It's the way in which we use it that can be bad. And that's our responsibility. **We can not attribute machines society's actions**.

Now, if a person is deciding to hurt someone through the internet, then **we can not blame the tool for this**. **We can not blame a tool** for the bad behaviour of some people.

The tool, all tools, are <u>positive in general</u> because they are trying to help us achieve something. **If** what we want to achieve is **bad**, we can **<u>not blame</u>** the tool for it.

65

My problem with the argumentation of the opposition is that basically they are giving us a list of the morally bad content available on the internet. OK. **But this is not the topic of the debate**. Moral is not the topic of the debate. **We could stand here as well and start talking about all the good things about the internet**. How it allows for freedom of speech, globalisation, **but if you understand the thesis**, it is **clear** that the point here is: "Does the internet help the user achieve what he wants?" **Yes, it does**. **Therefore**, we have proven that it is possible.

Now, what the user wants, is it always something morally good? **Unfortunately**, it isn't. But that is **not** what the thesis tells us that we must debate. The third speaker I think it was, you

**agreed** with our thesis. **You said that it was completely positive**. But you **confused** morally good with positive. **Therefore**, you have given us the **right** (*la razón*) here. **You said we are right, therefore, this is obvious**. Thank you very much for listening to me.

*** End of 4th & Final Proposition Speech

4th Opposition Speaker: Nolvia Collao  (3 minutes – Summary Speech)

(Nolvia delivers her speech **standing behind the podium**, with a microphone)

"Good afternoon everyone. My name is Nolvia. From all the arguments you have heard here today, **we** can **surely conclude** that the internet, **is not a positive influence** on society. **Firstly**, the internet **harms** participation in social life and social relationships. Studies showed greater use of the internet was **significantly associated with** decreased communication within the family. Decreased local social networks. Loneliness and depression. **Contradicting** the proposition's **claim** that the internet **increases social contact.**

We told you that 1 in 8 Americans suffers from internet addictions, **but do you remember the consequences?** Internet addicts **suffer** from academic and social problems. Developed physical illnesses. Lose excessive amounts of money. Neglect significant relationships.

Secondly, the Proposition (Team) talked about children going on the net for educational purposes. **But in fact**, the internet is an almost perfect medium for offenders seeking children for sex. Pedophiles use the internet to stalk unsupervised children in chat rooms. I remind you, that the UK police claimed there can be over 50 thousand predators prowling the internet – at-any-given-time (*softly said*). This also means that bullies can also torment, threaten, harrass, humiliate, and embarrass their victims ( Nolvia's *tone of voice drops*). 24 hours a day – 7 days a week, having **deadly consequences**.

**Thirdly**, the internet has broken down the traditional barriers to crime. In the past, the culprit had to be physically present to commit a crime. Now, cyber crimes can be committed from anywhere in the world. In 2006, alone, the internet fraud resulted in losses of 198 Million Dollars. (*Nolvia steps down from the podium, with microphone in hand*)

**The Proposition told us** that you can communicate with anyone in the world. And it's **true**. **However**, there is **no denying** that Al Qaeda authorities communicated with each other on the internet. In planning and coordinating the 2001, September 11 attacks in New York. Ladies and Gentlemen: Do you think that facilitating one of the **worst** terrorist attacks in history, **is a positive influence on society**?

**In conclusion**, the internet has brought about <u>social isolation</u> <u>and addictions</u>. It provides <u>anonymity for sexual predators</u>, and <u>cyber bullies abuse children</u>, and <u>cyber crime has resulted in</u> <u>hundreds of millions of dollars in losses</u>. [ *Nolvia has dropped the microphone away from her mouth, uses her natural voice, and shouts*: ] CLEARLY – THIS IS NOT A POSITIVE INFLUENCE ON SOCIETY! Thank you very much.

\*\*\* With this the debate is ended.

\*\*\* The Judges' decision, announced by Minister Jimenez: **<u>11 votes to 10</u>**.

The Winner: Colegio Santa Emilia de Antofagasta!

**Exercise:** Tick the boxes "Yes" or "No", for each speech.

| Evaluation / Analysis of 2nd Speeches: | | |
|---|---|---|
| **Category** | **Amanda Labarca** | **Santa Emilia** |
| | | |
| Opening Statement | | |
| Speaker Style | | |
| Team Strategy | | |
| Rebuild Arguments | | |
| Research Points | | |
| Summary | | |
| SignalPhrase Signpost | | |
| Inclusive Pronoun We/Us | | |
| Argumentation (AREL) | | |
| Rebuttal "wrong" | | |
| Contrast Differentiation | | |
| Team Line | | |
| Audibility | | |
| Engagement | | |
| Conviction | | |
| Authority | | |
| Likability | | |
| FairPlay (Squirrel) | | |
| Timing (3 minutes) | | |
| Comments Remarks | | |

**Exercise:** Using the chart below, tick the boxes "Yes" or "No".

| Category | Amanda La Barca  | Santa Emilia  |
|---|---|---|
| **Evaluation / Analysis of 3rd Speeches:** | | |
| | | |
| Opening Statement | | |
| Speaker Style | | |
| Team Strategy | | |
| Rebuild Arguments | | |
| Research Points | | |
| Summary | | |
| SignalPhrase Signpost | | |
| Inclusive Pronoun We/Us | | |
| Argumentation (AREL) | | |
| Rebuttal "wrong" | | |
| Contrast Differentiation | | |
| Team Line | | |
| Audibility | | |
| Engagement | | |
| Conviction | | |
| Authority | | |
| Likability | | |
| FairPlay (Squirrel) | | |
| Timing (3 minutes) | | |
| Comments Remarks | | |

**Exercise:** Using the chart below, tick the boxes "Yes" or "No".

| Evaluation / Analysis of 4th Speeches: | | |
|---|---|---|
| **Category** | **Amanda Labarca**  | **Santa Emilia**  |
| | | |
| Opening Statement | | |
| Speaker Style | | |
| Team Strategy | | |
| Rebuild Arguments | | |
| Research Points | | |
| Summary | | |
| SignalPhrase Signpost | | |
| Inclusive Pronoun We/Us | | |
| Argumentation (AREL) | | |
| Rebuttal "wrong" | | |
| Contrast Differentiation | | |
| Team Line | | |
| Audibility | | |
| Engagement | | |
| Conviction | | |
| Authority | | |
| Likability | | |
| FairPlay (Squirrel) | | |
| Timing (3 minutes) | | |
| Comments Remarks | | |

## Debate Analysis :WSDC New Zealand VS Chile
Video of the debate: http://vimeo.com/7490164

| Evaluation / Analysis of 1st Speeches: | | |
|---|---|---|
| Category | New Zealand - James | Chile - Domingo |
| | | |
| Introduction | | |
| Motion | | |
| Team Strategy | | |
| Team Split | | |
| "We will prove" | | |
| Key terms | | |
| Signal phrase | | |
| Inclusive Pronoun | | |
| AREL | | |
| Rebuttal "wrong" | | |
| Contrast Differentiation | | |
| Team Line | | |
| Audibility | | |
| Engagement | | |
| Conviction | | |
| Authority | | |
| Likability | | |
| Fair Play (Squirrel) | | |
| Time: (8minutes) minutes) | | |

# WSDC DEBATE TRANSCRIPT:

# NEW ZEALAND VS CHILE

The purpose of this exercise is to evaluate the speeches from the 2009 Mini-WSDC in Doha, Qatar. The two teams participating in the Final Round are New Zealand and Chile.
The Motion is: **THBT a country should not punish those who pay bribes to officials of other countries**:
1<sup>st</sup> Proposition Speaker: James Penn (8 minutes)
(James delivers his speech **standing behind the podium**, with a microphone)

James: "In 2003, the UK Serious Fraud Office, started an investigation into the allegations of bribes, paid by British Aerospace (BAE), to the Saudi Royal Family. And these allegations, - were in exchange - what were - the bribes were paid in exchange for arms deals that went on to be Britain's largest ever export. In 2006, this inquest was abolished by the British government.

Here on Team New Zealand today, we think this was for some very good reasons. We think that if the inquest had gone ahead, and that the bribes were um, were found to be true, then we think that this would have had very big **negative effects** um, **on the foreign** relationship with um, **the Saudi government and the Saudi Royal Family**. Um, **which is what I'm going to be talking about** today. **I'm also going to be talking about** how when you start to punish individuals who pay bribes to officials of other countries, you get what is called, **"Cultural Imperialism"** and then **Nick (Nicholas Orr) is gonna come out as second (speaker) and talk about the certain economic harms that come about when countries start to punish their own citizens for paying bribes** to um, officials of other countries.

Now here on Side Proposition, we think **it's important to define this motion**. We define it to mean that um, in terms of the U – taking the UK example, that any citizen of Britain would not be prosecuted by the British government for bribing government officials of other countries. We think that, um, we would suggest this in Britain, we think that we would also suggest other governments all around the world to take up this um, this – this – um – this model and to stop – um – and-and would not prosecute their citizens for this sort of thing either.

So, on to my first **substantive** (argument) about the **impact** it would have on foreign policy. Now if a government starts getting involved and hindering deals between companies in countries, by punishing the company, it has effects on the other side of the deal, on the country. We see this to um, we see this to the effect the one country starts to get annoyed with the other country for doing this and implementing these punishments and this ruins the deal. And the - and the country doesn't - isn't – um – in fact in favor of this obviously because they are not getting their side of the bargain, they're not getting um, their side of the deal that they wanted. So what we see as a result of this is that we start to get um hindrances to foreign relations between the governments.

And we see this – we see **an example** of this in the case of um, of the Saudi government and the BAE example. And as – um – what happened with the deals called "Al Yamana" (???) weapons deals. They began in the 1985s (sic), they went right through the present day. They're still ongoing and we um ["*Point of Information*" (Paulina – refused by James)] in the first 20 years these deals worth um 43 Milli- uh Billion pounds. These were massive deals to Britain but they are also massive deals to the Saudi Royal Family. And another deal – um - for a further forty million pounds worth of deals was um happening.

Now, we see that when the government started this inquest, into these bribes and they started to investigate into these allegations of the bribes, the Saudi gover – uh the Saudi Royal Family didn't like us. And they responded by threatening to cut 6 Billion pounds worth of deals for Eurospace fighters, but more importantly, they started to respond by threatening to cut all um all sharing of terrorist intelligence that they had. And we see that this sort of thing to – would be replicated um in many other deals if the individuals were punished. And we see that foreign relations in many other areas around the world would be um – would be hindered by punishing individuals of your own country – um – for paying bribes to officials [ "*Sir*"(POI offered by Domingo

Carbone – accepted by James)] of other countries. **<u>Wouldn't you agree</u>**?

Domingo: "By this excuse of happiness, would you actually go against the law? Would you actually break it to bring happiness..."

James: "**<u>I get your point</u>**. No, what we think, firstly, we think that the law shouldn't have been there - that's why we're standing up here debating today, but moreover we think that um the law shouldn't have been there [*"Point of Information"* (Paulina – rejected by James. He motions for Paulina to sit down)] because we think these foreign relations take precedent over the bribes and we don't think the bribes actually do the huge amount of harm that we've heard – uh – that the Opposition thinks – **that they're probably going to come up here and start arguing today**.

Now, we think that – um – the British, the British government took very good steps and um – in terms of stopping these inquests and we think that it was an effective way to do things because they weighed up the costs to their – to the sharing of terrorist intelligence – to the benefits they would get by punishing these individuals. [*"Point of Information"* (Paulina - rejected by James again)] Now, we also think um that British government uh were brave to look at the <u>harms versus the benefits</u> and could weigh these up and were able to see that the foreign relations and that the sharing of terrorist infor – um – intelligence was very – uh – should take precedent and was more important to society and to the country. [*"Point of Information"* (Paulina – this time James accepts the POI)] **Wouldn't you agree?**

Paulina (standing): "**<u>No, I wouldn't agree</u>**. So, what you're saying is that corruption is actually not bad enough. Am I understanding your point?"

James: "Um, no. We think corruption isn't necessarily a great thing but we don't think it's really a bad thing either and we think that foreign relations obviously had to take precedent and I don't think that foreign relations in these sort of instances aren't more important and we don't think that intelligence on terrorists actions that the Saudi governm – that the Saudi Royal Family have are more important to Britain and in this case they didn't and that punishing the individuals through um – that these deals and we stil think that these foreign relations would be hindered and many other deals that would be cancelled as a result of – um – punishing other – punishing individuals for paying bribes to officials of other countries.

So, now **on to my second substantive** (argument) "Cultural Imperialism". That is demonstrated when a country starts to – um – punishing individuals who pay bribes to officials of other countries. Now what **this means** is that a country starts to impose their values and their policies on other countries just because their citizens are doing something legal in those countries.

But I think the British government wouldn't punish an individual if they went over to Holland and smoked some marijuana. Because it's legal over there. I think these values should be replicated in terms of paying bribes because when it happens in other country, it doesn't – um – become the British responsibility and we think that the British don't have a place in opposing their policy, their values, and their laws on this country. ["*Sir*" (Domingo offers a POI – rejected by James)]

Now, we think that these – that these is – um - that-that these cultural values are very important to countries because they have historical precedence and several historical and cultural standing in these countries. Over the centuries, these traditions have been built up. Some countries – um – might see these – might see things such as – um – taking gifts – allowing – uh – uh-uh an official to stay at your very nice house so that um ["*Point of Information*" (Paulina – rejected by James sternly, saying: **"You're out of order"**)] um – we think that these – we think that these values and traditions are very important to a country – and once the country that is punishing the individual starts to impose this - **that is morally wrong**.

So, Ladies and Gentlemen we see that the example like BAE and South Asia it comes as charity tipping – it's – um – to receive favors and deals – um – with officials and with um executives of companies and the like. Now, some nations would see this as bribery but we think that it's actually tradition, important to the country, and we don't think that other governments have a place imposing their laws and their religion on these countries.

So Ladies and Gentlemen, **because we think that punishing individuals that pay bribes to other countries is a demonstration of cultural imperialism, because we think it**

**hinders foreign relationships**, and **because we think it has economic harms, we proudly beg to propose.**

*** End of 1st Proposition Speech

1st Opposition Speaker: Domingo Carbone (8 minutes)

(Domingo delivers his speech **standing behind the podium**, with a microphone.)

Domingo Carbone: "Ladies and Gentlemen, <u>what is the real problem today?</u> <u>What are we debating here?</u> <u>We're debating bribery.</u> Bribery is a **harm** that **we**, as the opposition team, firmly believe, we can **not** allow. It has **consequences** that are both **harmful** and **self-perpetuating**. And **this must be stopped**. The Proposition Team came here today with interesting notions. Such as culture. Such as traditions. Such as religion. Why some cultures may allow this. Bribery. The thing is, those are not really the **reasons** for bribery to exist. Those are **occasions** for bribery to happen. The thing is, the only reason bribery exists, is because **people are willing to pay**. And that is why, we firmly believe, that throughout the world, [(**Domingo proposes a counter plan here** – Team Chile has "gone on offense")] **there should be an agreement on no more bribery**. How do we plan to do this? We plan a slight **change** to the **status quo**. We plan on adhering to international standards. Standards approved by everyone so that there won't be any problem. Of what should – 1 - [*"On That Point Sir"* (James Penn offers a POI – Domingo ignores the POI completely)] (Point) Number 1 - What should – (point number) 1 - be considered as a bribe on agreement? And (point number) 2 – The **due process** of trial of the person **prosecuted**. We think that these people should be tried in their own countries [*"But Sir"* (James Penn gently insists on a POI – Domingo turns to James and says: "Not right now. Thank you very much". At the same time, Domingo motions for James to sit down)] in the nation where they committed the crime.

**What I'll do today is first rebut** most of their arguments on the Opposition Side, **and then**, give <u>our first two arguments</u> on the Proposition Side, which are: **First**, that their, the reasons punishing – um – corruption at home and not elsewhere are only right to be applied and that, (number) **Two**: Economic and social consequences can not be continued [*"Sir"* (Nicholas Orr offers a

POI – Domingo rejects by saying: "Not right now, thank you very much". )]

The third argument and the fourth argument will be done by our second speaker, Paulina. Which are: First, corruption vies for legal power elsewhere, something that is not what we should have. We should stay within our own boundaries and that Two - It actually works! It is an accurate assertion that will be applied and actually **it is in use right now**.

**On to my first substantive point**, will be – uh – **rebuttal**. The Proposition came to you today, with the notion of foreign relationships – of being friends with the people around us. ["*Point of Information Sir*" (Tim Robinson offers a POI – Domingo refuses: "Not right now, thank you very much. He motions for Tim to sit down.)]

Corruption, is it a great thing? <u>They agreed</u>. They do not recognise a problem in corruption. **And we want to point that to the entire audience**. There is a **problem**, and the **Proposition** (Team) **knows it**. <u>**They know it, and they accept it**</u>. But they think, - intelligence - and that was most of their first speech, is more important. **We do not think so**. And we will prove to you today that that is wrong. Here are the reasons ["*But Sir*" (James tries again – Domingo rejects him: "Not right now".)]

**Now, concerning foreign relations,** there is such a thing as **sovereignty**. I am on to my banners (??). The reason why I'm Chilean is because I am from my country and I should stay in my country. Any power I might have there. On the political level ["*On That Point*" (Nicholas tries to ask a POI – Domingo ignores him. )] should stay in that country. If I have no nationality whatsoever in a country, I should not be able to travel. And that is exactly the point that Paulina will prove in our second speech.

Criminals come from another country, they do not come from the country itself. And they should be punished in the country where they come from. Why is this right? It is right, because we, as an Opposition Team, stand for the extra-territoriality. ["*Sir*" (Tim Robinson tries to ask a POI but Domingo ignores him)] We mean that this crime is actually happening in two places at the same time: the place where it's coming from, and the country of origin, which in most cases in this kind of debate, we're talking about countries with a lot of money, a lot of resources, and the country where it's happening: Countries that are extremely poor. A point that we will continue on our debate. Yes. (Domingo has accepted a POI)

James Penn: "Sir, **is it really worth** imposing our values when this could lose us valuable intel on terrorists?"

Domingo: "We are not imposing anything here. That is why we proposed an agreement. And intelligence really is **not as important as the value of human life**. [*"On That Point Sir"* (James tries again – Domingo answers: "Not right now. Thank you very much.")]

**Crimes should be punished**. And thing is, when it comes to this kind of bribery, the person that is actually bribing, is not the one that is punished in the country itself. What we mean is that, bigger CEOs come from a couch in New York, in Boston, whatever, and sending people in places like Guinea and they don't have to [*"On That Point Sir"* (Nicholas asks for a POI – Domingo ignores him)] travel themselves but the people they send are small executives and they won't get punished (Domingo turns and says. "Not right now. Thank you very much." while motioning for someone to sit down on the opposition team). It's not them, it's those small executives. The real fish, the one that is really committing the crime, are at home. And there are examples: Wal-Mart, IBM, Siemens, Architect In China, that is, from 2003 to 2008, these are some examples of the 74% of cases of corruption where international trade and foreign businesses were involved in cases. This is happening. It is a problem that is real and it should be stopped right now. (Not right now, thank you very much.)

And then there's the economic and social problem. Bribery undermines nations, economically throughout. Three Points. First, the external problem. This evil is undermining competition, for it creates an unlevel playing field. With an unstable and un --- (unintelligible) situation, scaring foreigner investors out. [*"But Sir"* (Nicholas Orr tries for a POI – Domingo ignores him)] We mean that, (*Domingo's voice dripping with sarcasm*) "<u>Why do I even try to do my best in order to achieve some business in a country, when anyone willing to pay a bribe will get the prize instead of me</u>? Or maybe, I'll get the prize, and I've already started on my investment - and then comes someone paying bribes that causes me to lose my money! I will not invest in that country!

["*Sir*" (It's Tim again – Domingo ignores him )] And that is why most countries with bribery are very poor. And that'll be our last point today.

My last point in this speech. There is no incentive, and that is our second case, to improve our products, as really but modest (unintelligible) now, in this economy, is actually paying the most price to the briber. It's not about the people buying the best product, or the best service, it's about me paying the best price to the best bidder. And that is wrong. These are not services. This is just nervous (?) consumers. And that is not right. (Domingo says this with a touch of sarcasm in his voice – emphasising two words – "that" and "not" for an extra millisecond, never breaking his delivery or rhythm) ["*Sir*" (James Penn again. – Domingo accepts the POI: "Yes")]

James Penn: "What about countries where bribery is part of cultural practice?"

Domingo: "Well, actually, there are no countries where bribery by itself is part of culture. But they say it's gifting. And **this** particular example actually refers to China. In China, what you do is a gift, not bribes. Everyone can tell from those small gift to a 1000 to a million dollar bill. It is not the same as gifts. Checks are not gifts. And I think people are smart enough to tell one from aother. Internally, local and national businessmen are at harm. They have no access to the amount of money they need to pay bribes, and thus the **internal** economy of these countries is hurt.

But I've told you about these poor countries. What poor countries am I talking about? I'm talking about countries with a lack, with the highest rates of corruption around the world. Which are: Uzbekistan, Afghanistan, Chad, Equatorial Guinea. What do you see in these countries? Foreigners. There is an economical consequence. And we should not allow it to keep on. And so it is, Ladies and Gentlemen, that we, the Opposition Side, come to the end of our first speech, and **because we've proven that this corruption is so harmful, economically and socially,** (*ting – a bell sounds – signalling time is up*) and **because punishment is necessary**, and **because it's imperative to act now, <u>we beg to oppose</u>**."

*** End of 1st Opposition Speech

85

**Exercise: Ticking the Boxes – Second Speeches**
Video of the debate: http://vimeo.com/7490164

| Evaluation / Analysis of 2$^{nd}$ Speeches: | | |
|---|---|---|
| **Category** | **Team New Zealand – Nicholas Orr** | **Team Chile - Paulina Valenzuela** |
| Opening: Begin Speech | | |
| Rebuttal each argument. | | |
| Signpost Language | | |
| 1$^{st}$Argument: A-R-E-L (Impact) | | |
| 2$^{nd}$Argument: A-R-E-L (Impact) | | |
| SpeechSummary | | |
| Team Line | | |
| Audibility | | |
| Engagement | | |
| Conviction | | |
| Authority | | |
| Likability | | |
| Content | | |
| TeamStrategy | | |
| Timing | | |
| Rebuild Arguments | | |
| Research Evidence | | |
| | | |

2nd Proposition Speaker: Nicholas Orr   (8 minutes)

(Nicholas delivers his speech **standing behind the podium**, with a microphone.)

Nicholas Orr: "When punishing those who pay bribes to officials of other countries, means imposing our own values on those other countries, in what is called, Cultural Imperialsim. When it means ignoring all the huge importance of foreign policy to countries, and the huge harms that can result, from not having good foreign policies, as James presented to you today, we say, on Side Proposition, we can not sacrifice those things, at the expense of dealing with some individual cases of corruption.

I've got two (2) substantive poins to present to you today, which are, The Economic Benefits of keeping what Side Proposition has put forth, and also, The Importance of the effect on poor countries.

But first, **I'm going to deal with** some of the major problems in the Side Opposition's case.

Because, they've come up here today and put one major, they've come up with one basic argument (*ting, a bell sounds indicating one minute has gone by)* ["*Point of Information*" (Paulina offers a POI – Nicholas ignores her)] which has a major flaw in it.  And we have told you that <u>international standards can not be agreed on</u>. Because everyone in the world has different cultural values and different cultural and legal policies.  ["*Point of Information*" (Paulina offers a POI – Nicholas ignores her)] Now, when they come up here and say, "We're going to agree to some sort of international standards",  considering that James did in most of his speech, telling you how we can't – uh – come up with these sorts of – uh – integrating policies, **we see that this can not possibly work,** what Side Opposition has said.  Um – also, <u>they have put forth</u> this kind of **countermodel** type thing, with this idea that – uh – **gifts aren't included as bribes**.   <u>We say</u> this is just like evidently **wrong, because** – uh – **gifts are considered bribes** in many countries.  **Look at** the USA and New Zealand, **gifts to political parties are just straight illegal**. (*Domingo is standing to offer a POI* ["*Sir*" (barely audible) – Nicholas ignores him)] – Now, uh, because we've already shown you cultural – how we must respect cultural differences, and because we must keep our cultural differences that exist between societies, we say, and we can't undermine the sovereignty (*Domingo is drinking water, Valentina runs her hands through her hair, Paulina is looking at her notes*) of other countries, we say, that we won't stand for cultural imperialism (*Nicholas speaks these lines without passion – almost a monotone*).

I'm going to move on to some of these things they said about the problems with corruption, (*Valentina is standing to offer a POI – hands on hips*) so **even if** this sort of **counter-model** would work, there are some major things I need to address. And they've come up here and said (*Valentina sits back down*) that we "need to combat corruption" (*Domingo rises to offer a POI* ["*Sir*" (barely audible again) – Nicholas ignores him)] but we say it's going to be unfair. (*Domingo writes a note on his notepad and sits down*) Certainly – um – to bring about this – uh – to start making these plans because cultural – uh – cultural differences exist. And different traditions (" *Point Of Information, Sir*" [ (Paula's voice booms loudly and confidently) – Nicholas ignores her)] exist in different countries and they have different perceptions of what "corruption" means. And we showed you the BAE example. (" *Point Of Information, Sir*" [ (Paula's voice booms loudly and confidently) – Nicholas ignores her)] A universal by which we can evaluate the legality of actions, it would be unfair to impose on individuals things which are considered culturally practiceable (" *Point Of Information, Sir*" [ (Domingo's voice booms loudly and confidently) – Nicholas ignores him)] in their countries. To illustrate this, **just imagine** citizens of other countries, coming to your own country, engaging in institutionalised practices, and then being prosecuted at home. **First and foremost**, you would consider this **morally wrong** (" *Point Of Information, Sir*" [ (Paula's voice booms loudly and confidently) – Nicholas ignores her)] **so this issue falls outside of the house.**

But **secondly**, we think that this industry would be destroyed and - **I'll Take You In A Moment** – (*Nicholas indicates he will accept a POI from the opposition team when he finishes making his current point*) this industry would be destroyed in your own country with a lot of anger and economic harms to show and also

(" *Point Of Information,* " [ (Domingo's voice booms loudly)] such as in Saudi Arabia. Yes, I'll take your question.

Domingo Carbone: "Bribery is legal everywhere in the world. The problem is, it's not in force, the law is not being enforced. What do you say to that?"

(*All the members of Team Chile look at Nicholas expectantly, knowing it was a good question. Nicholas hesitates for a moment before answering, trying desperately to think of an answer that will **"turn the tables"** , that is, to try to use Doningo's question against him.)

Nicholas asks for clarification: "You saying that bribery is not – bribery is illegal..."

Domingo interrupts to clarify: "Bribery is **illegal** almost everwhere around the world. The problem is enforcement."

Nicholas: "Well, we're saying that we gonna keep – like – we agree that corruption is bad. But, we say that, sometimes, things like foreign policy, mean that we must – um – eh – keep these – these things going. And cultural imposition means that we must keep these things going. So, we think this is clearly wrong."

(*Nicholas has given a purely defensive answer – defending his team's position – without being able to use the question against the proposition team.)

Nicholas continues: "Now, **they didn't address** what James provided about foreign policy.   We think that it's incredibly important to ensure the sharing of terrorist information, in the Saudi Arabian example.   This could produce a **huge harm** to the UK **as a direct example** of this.

**I'm also going to move on to my substantive (arguments for my position) now**, the economic problems which would occur as a result of these foreign policy changes.   And – OK.   On to economic problems.   The impacts on British jobs would be tremendous if we – um - [" *Point Of Information*" (Paulina offers a POI – Nicholas ignores her)]   put this into place.   Industries would be destroyed.   Let's look at the facts.   43 Billion pounds - (*Paulina stands and speaks into the microphone forcefully*) [" *Point Of Information, Sir*" (Paula offers a POI – Nicholas ignores her)] would be lost in the first 20 years. (*Paulina remains standing – indicating she will not accept being ignored. POI etiquette requires Nicholas to accept, or refuse, the POI – he has done neither*)

Nicholas continues: "From these – from the BAE contract with Saudia Arabia.   And it was the overall largest ever export for – um – England.   And so look at the impacts on the masses, the masses of people (*Paulina leans forward and speaks into the microphone on her table*) [" *Point Of Information, Sir.* ")]

Nicholas responds without looking at her:  "I'll Take You In A Minute. (He has accepted Paulina's POI.  He will take her question after he finishes with the point he is making – **which must occur as soon as he finishes making his current point – usually no more than 10 to 15 seconds**)  if those jobs are lost.  Um – Regarding those jobs, if you just lose all these jobs in a society there will be a huge economic downturn. So we can not allow this to happen, and that is why foreign policy must come first. Yes. (*Now Paulina can ask*)

Paulina Valenzuela: "You **insist** about countries' sovereignty, and how we shouldn't disrespect it, **however**, eh, corruption and bribery only **undermine** the **sovereignty**".

*** *Dear Reader, Nicholas is perplexed, and well he should be.*

*Why? Paulina has not asked a question, but she has made a* **brilliant** *statement which seeks to trap Nicholas.*

*Her statement tempts Nicholas to answer: " Yes, sovereignty is a good thing for a country, and No, corruption and bribery do not undermine sovereignty".*

*It is a <u>contradictory</u> position - the idea that national sovereignty is good and it <u>is not</u> affected by corruption and bribery - and thus it would be an easy argument for Paulina to win – if Nicholas falls for the trap.*

*On the other hand, if Nicholas <u>denies</u> that his team is insisting on sovereignty for countries to practice their culture and traditions – he <u>will contradict</u> what he and James Penn have already said about respecting countries' sovereign right to accept bribery as a business practice in their country.*

*Dear Reader: How would YOU answer Paulina's question?\*\*\**

[ <u>Answer Paulina's question before you turn the page to read what Nicholas' answer was</u> ]

## A Dilemma for Nicholas

Nicholas responds: "Um – corruption is not undermining sovereignty because it's – Corruption is not undermining sovereignty at all.  Because we basically addressed this, Ladies and Gentlemen, because of the simple facts about uh – removing foreign policies and cultural imposition on these countries, which we can not allow.

So, **I'm going to move on** also to this idea of the – um – uh the – impacts on these poor countries – with - um – public servants – that um – basically yeah – about public servants.  Because in many countries, public servants – in many poor countries of the world,

public servants only way of getting a real income   is like –
**through these bribes**.  Because it's not enough money to help
them.  It's not enough money provided (*ting, a bell sounds –
Nicholas has one minute left in his speech*) by the government to
give them a good job.  And so, we think, that because they will
only be able to continue to exist through the bribes which are – um
– important, through the bribes which are brought in occasionally,
and although there are some harms with these bribes, yes we admit
that, but, the fact is, we would be destroying the jobs for all these
public servants.  Otherwise they simply wouldn't be able to exist.
And we say, that, – Is it better to have a government that is
completely destroyed by – um – by – removing all these – uh –
cross-country transactions (?) or – Is it better to – um – Is it better
to have – yeah – Government which is destroyed by cross-country
transactions or one which doesn't accept corruption but
nevertheless, that keeps a firm government in place, that can keep
a stable country going?  And we believe that this is definitely true.
So, (*ting-ting, the bell sounds twice – Nicholas' time is up – he
must finish in the next ten seconds or he will lose points for going
over the time limit*) because of the terrible impacts of cultural
imposition, and the terrible impacts of foreign policy that this
would result in, -uh – **the moot (motion) must stand today**.
*** End of 2$^{nd}$ Proposition Speech

2nd Opposition Speaker: Paulina Valenzuela   (8 minutes)
(Paulina delivers her speech **standing behind the podium**, with
a microphone.)

Paulina Valenzuela: "Good afternoon, Ladies and Gentlemen.
Today, the Proposition (Team) has come here with an interesting
assertion: "Corruption Is Not That Bad".  So, what they're saying
is that this problem is not bad enough as to handle it in an
appropriate way.  However, when "Transparency International" –
ur – gives this report, saying, "that out of 159 countries, that bad
evaluated, 134 have serious corruption problems".  We can't say
with certainty that there is a lot of harm.  Corruption is a problem,
and bribery is one of the main components of corruption.  So, the
opposition here (*she means Team Chile*) is standing for something

that goes against this corruption. Because, unlike what the Proposition (*Team NZ*) thinks, this is very bad for the world and it damages it.

Today, I will present you a case, first, by **rebutting** two main arguments given by the Proposition. Cultural differences must be respected, (*ting, the bell sounds, indicating one minute has gone by - now the other team can begin to ask PI's*) country sovereignty, and then [*"On That Point", (Tim Robinson asks a POI – Paulina refuses and motions for Tim to sit down)*] by rebuilding, **by rebuilding the arguments** given by Domingo, about economic harm, and a crime is committed in two countries at a time. And then I will present you our **last two arguments** – that is – That Corruption Buys Political Power. And then, these laws utterly(?) work.

**First of all**, cultural differences must be respected. Ladies and Gentlemen, corruption, everywhere(!) in this world (Paulina raised her voice dramatically on the word – *everywhere* – and then decreased the volume) is illegal. Corruption [*"Ma'am", (Tim Robinson tries to ask a POI – Paulina refuses and motions for Tim to sit down)*] everywhere in this world, is seen as something bad. What is different, and what differs from country to country, is what a bribe is considered. Because some people consider that a gift is a bribe, and some people don't. (Paulina *"waves off"* another POI attempt, motioning for the person to sit down) But we have already dealt with this problem by telling you, that this law that we are proposing here, that we're saying it should be enforced, would define clearly, what a bribe is, so that these confusions won't be produced.

Two, we don't understand what you're saying with your thing of cultural differences. (*"Ma'am"* – softly spoken over the microphone – refused by Paulina with a motion to sit down) Every country in this world accepts that bribery and corruption is wrong. Well, the thing happens here is that individuals don't want to harm their own pockets. (*Paulina taps her right pocket as she says this*). And we can't start worrying about people's pockets here. [*" Point of Information, Ma'am", (Tim Robinson asks a POI – Paulina turns to the speaker and accepts the POI)*] Yes.

Tim Robinson: "Ma'am, have you ever heard about the cultural practice of Bakshish?"

Paulina: "What?"

Tim repeats: "Ma'am, have you ever heard of the cultural practice of Bakshish? That's what we brought out in our first speech."

Paulina: "Cultural differences of countries considered to small aspects are not enough. Because there's no one who can [("*But Ma'am – Nicholas disagrees with Paulina's answer – Paulina motions for him to sit down* )] There's no one who can say, that "Corruption is something good". There is no one who can say that undermining the authority of someone by paying him, is good. **So, we don't think this is a valid argument**.

Now, about country sovereignty, this team is saying here that we would damage country sovereignty because of the extra-territoriality [(*"On That Point"* – Paulina motions for the person to sit down)] However, **the only thing that corruption and bribery does is undermining the sovereignty of a country. Because it implies buying political power**. And this will be further explained in one of my arguments. [(*"Ma'am – It's James Penn – Paulina accepts the POI* )] Yes.

James Penn: Do you think that one country imposing their set of laws on another countries' policies that are based on cultural values is undermining sovereignty?"

*** *James has asked an excellent question, of which the only rational answer would be – Yes. If answered affirmatively, Paulina becomes guilty of doing the same thing that she has accused Team NZ of, namely, undermining the sovereignty of a country.****

Paulina responds: "Cultural values. So, you're actually saying that culture values corruption? A gift, Sir, is not the same that (sic) a bribe. There is a lot of difference between me giving you a chocolate for your birthday, or giving you a 25 thousand dollar big check. Because I want you to buy my business. And [(*Ma'am – Paulina motions James to sit down*)] nobody can be that naíve, as to believe that someone can confuse a gift by (sic) a check. This is totally naive and it's justifying a problem that is serious. [(*"On That Point, Ma'am" James requests a POI – Paulina refuses, saying: "No thank you."*)]

Now, **going to my arguments**. First of all, **Domingo told you about** economic harms involved in bribery. Economic harms include that a country, that has a lot of corruption and bribery, is eliminating an even competition between companies. When a company is more, cares more and is putting in more money in to having better bribes than better products, then they have a problem. If I'm doing a great product, other countries are not buying it because my competitor is giving a bad product but a good bribe, then we have a problem. And this is economic harm. So, [(*"Ma'am" Tim requests a POI – Paulina refuses, by motioning for him to sit down."*)] are saying here, we would eliminate commercial transactions between countries? No we wouldn't. We would just be doing it much more fair, and thus, we would be helping the market. So, what you're saying is not valid. We don't think it's valid because an economic transaction that is based on a market that is totally full of failures, it is not right.

Now, [(*"Ma'am" Tim requests a POI – Paulina refuses, by motioning for him to sit down."*)] **about buying political power**. How corruption and bribery undermine the sovereignty of a country. When an officer's main issue is to deal with citizen's problems and solve them. However, when he cares more about his own pocket than about the worries of everyone else, we have a problem, **don't we?** Let me give you an example of Guinea. Exxon started investing in Guinea, and eh, [(*"Point Ma'am" Nicholas requests a POI – Paulina refuses, motions for him to sit down*)] No thank you. And giving money to the Guinea government so as to be able to exploit the petroleum that was in the area. What happened? This money was given as a bribe. And not as a payment for the government. So, - thuuu – dictator of Guinea just put that money in his pocket. So, while he's rich and has a lot of money, 70% of the Guinean population is under the line of poverty. , [(*"Point Ma'am" Nicholas requests a POI – Paulina refuses, motions for him to sit down*)]

This only harms the Guinean economy and its credibility around the world, and thus, sovereignty. A country is not ruling itself, because in this case, Exxon is ruling. Because the governor of Guinea wants to have his money, right? So, he will only do what Exxon is telling him to do. This happens [(" *Ma'am" James requests a POI – Paulina refuses, motions for him to sit down*)] in many cases. When you are receiving money from someone, you do as you (sic) tells you to do. [*** correction - *you do as you are told to do*] Because you want to still receive that money. So, the thing they're saying about sovereignty is not right. The legality (?) of this law is totally justified. When you're bribing someone else, you're damaging your own country and crime Doming told you [(*"Point Ma'am" Tim requests a POI – Paulina refuses, motions for him to sit down*)] the crime is not committed in just the country where you pay the bribe, it's committed in your own country. Because the intellectual planning of that crime was committed in your country (*ting, the bell sounds – Paulina has one more minute*) Because the money comes from your country. And the Proposition said, **it's impossible to enforce**, this is not true. It is actually being enforced by the OECD Treaty, by the Foreign Corrupt Practice of the US. For example, in Germany it's being enforced and Siemens employees, thanks to this law, came forward to openly recrimination about Siemens, making able to prove that Siemens had – eh – corrupted countries such as Nigeria, and now is being fined 306 Million Dollars. So, these laws actually work. And why do they work Ladies and Gentlemen? Why? Because people are worried about corruption. Because we don't want to have corrupt governments. Because we don't want that disadvantages of people to be – eh – over one another, not because of their capacities, but because of their ability to pay a bigger bribe. We think that what the Proposition is telling you here is (*ting-ting, Paulina's time is up, she must finish her speech in the next ten seconds*) totally immoral according to the values that we are trying to propose in our society. There's no culture that thinks that corruption is right. Thank you Very Much.

\*\*\* End of 2<sup>nd</sup> Opposition Speech

\*\*\* Dear Reader, let's analyse the speeches so far. What is happening in each speech?

The first speaker, 1<sup>st</sup> Proposition, James Penn, **introduced the motion** and **defined it**, giving a **model** from which the debate would be argued. Then he made his team's first **2 arguments to justify** his team's position. He also made a short **rebuttal** in general terms about the argument that he **anticipated** the Opposition Team would make.

Next, 1<sup>st</sup> Opposition speaker, Domingo Carbone, spoke. He introduced his team's **counter-plan**, then did **rebuttal** of the arguments made by James, and finished by making his 2 **arguments** for his team's position.

Next, 2<sup>nd</sup> Proposition speaker, Nicholas Orr, spoke. First, he did **rebuttal** of the arguments made by Domingo. After that, Nicholas **rebuilt** his team's **arguments**, saying why the criticisms of his team's arguments were **not valid**. Finally, Nicholas gave **2 new arguments** for his team's position.

Next, Paulina Valenzuela, 2<sup>nd</sup> Opposition speaker, came up and did **rebuttal** of the 2 new arguments made by Nicholas for his team's position.  Then she **rebuilt** her team's **arguments**, saying why the criticisms of Domingo's arguments, were **not valid**.

Finally, Paulina gave **2 new arguments** for her team's position.

Thus, both 2$^{nd}$ speeches have three main parts:

**Rebuttal – Rebuild – New Arguments**:

Thus, both 2$^{nd}$ speeches have three main parts:  Rebuttal – Rebuild – New Arguments:

| 1$^{st}$ Proposition – New Zealand (James) | 1$^{st}$ Opposition – Chile (Domingo) |
|---|---|
| Opening (to get audience attention) | Opening (to get audience attention) |
| Define the motion | Signpost Structure |
| Signpost Structure | Rebuttal of all 1$^{st}$ Prop Arguments |
| 2 Arguments | 2 Arguments |
| Summary | Summary |
| 2$^{nd}$ Proposition – (Nicholas) | 2$^{nd}$ Opposition – (Paulina) |
| Opening (to get audience attention) | Opening (to get audience attention) |
| Rebuttal of all 1$^{st}$ Opp Arguments | Rebuttal of all 2$^{nd}$ Prop Arguments |
| Rebuild | Rebuild |
| 2 New Arguments | 2 New Arguments |

***Now, let's continue on with the debate.***

3nd Proposition Speaker: Tim Robinson   (8 minutes)
(Tim delivers his speech **standing behind the podium**, with a microphone.)

Tim Robinson: "Ladies and Gentlemen, today the opposition case is mainly based on the whole idea between gifts and bribes. Ladies and Gentlemen, we see this as a bigger issue.  She said 25 thousand dollar check, versus a chocolate bar.  What about a 25 thousand dollar check, versus a 25 thouand dollar boat?  Ladies and Gentlemen, we say that gifts and bribes are essentially the same thing, and when you're giving a gift, as she said, for someone's birthday.  While she believes in a bribe as a token gesture of friendship, we say that gifts can be done as bribes.  And so we see that this is just a **stupid** point for them to be putting the crux of their case on."

*** Dear Reader, Tim just committed a serious mistake – using the word "stupid".  Every judge will relate the word "stupid" to mean "Team Chile **is** stupid", regardless whether Tim means that or not. Take note, Dear Reader: Tim Robinson has just demonstrated **how to make sure the judges do NOT like you and your team** – by using vocabulary that is <u>disrespectful</u> to the other team.***

****Ok, Dear Reader, you ask, "What about Paulina?" Yes, Paulina said Team New Zealand was "naive". However, consulting the Oxford Dictionary (2009), we find the word "naive" means: lacking experience of life, knowledge or good judgement, and willing to believe that people always tell you the truth.

For an example from history, let's look at what British Prime Minister Neville Chamberlain said after meeting with Adolf Hitler to discuss peace. PM Chamberlain said: "Yesterday afternoon I had a long talk with Herr Hitler. It was a frank talk, but it was a friendly one, and I feel satisfied now, that <u>each of us fully understands what is in the mind of the other</u>."

History would bear out that Prime Minister Chamberlain was indeed <u>naive</u>, but *not* <u>stupid</u>. Although he was mistaken about Hitler's intentions, PM Neville Chamberlain was able to delay the start of war with Germany, which resulted in Britain winning valuable time to prepare for the inevitable war that came.***

Tim Robinson continues: "When they could have been engaging with us, on some of our ideas, like foreign policy, <u>which they just completely missed</u>.

So Ladies and Gentlemen, <u>first of all</u>, I'm gonna have a look at their counter-model, which doesn't really do much to solve our problems, and *(ting, the bell sounds indicating one minute has passed – Team Chile can now ask POIs)* they stuff they are having with us. Not that it actually works. Then I'm going to [*("On That Point, Sir") – Paulina offers a POI – Tim looks over at her but refuses the POI)]* "No thank you, ma'am. Then I'm going to look at the fact that – uh – the fact of imposing cultural imperialism, the whole sovereignty [*("On That Point, Sir") – Again, Paulina offers a POI – Tim ignores her]* issue. Then, I'm going to look at – uh - the restriction of business, Ladies and Gentlemen.

So first of all, their counter-model. Now we say that they've come up here saying that they wouldn't dream of imposing legal power on a nation's sovereignty because this is what bribes do

Ladies and Gentlemen. But what about the fact that we have come up here today and we have said that New Zealand and the UK are allowed to pay – businesses are allowed to pay money to political parties? In the United States, only individual are allowed to pay money to political parties."

\*\*\* Please note: On January 21, 2010, the Supreme Court of the United States, on a vote of 5-4, upheld a ruling which allows businesses to pay money to political parties. President Obama commented: "The Supreme Court has given a green light to a new stampede of special interest money in our politics. It is a major victory for big oil, Wall Street banks, health insurance companies, and the other powerful interests that marshal their power every day in Washington to drown out the voices of everyday Americans."

Justice John Paul Stevens wrote: "The court's ruling threatens to undermine the integrity of elected institutions across the nation." In 2008, nearly 6 Billion dollars was spent on all federal election campaigns. (Source: Reuters News – James Vicini: Jan. 21, 2010).\*\*\*

Tim continues: "And Belgium, not at all. So Ladies and Gentlemen, at some stage when they (Team Chile) are making their big, happy international agreement, some country is going to be missing out. Ladies and Gentlemen, there are some countries that actually have compromised. And we say that this is harming a nation's sovereignty, and it should be up to the individual nations to choose if bribery is allowed or not. [("On That Point, Sir"Valentina Salvatiera offers a POI – Tim looks at her and refuses)] No thank you, ma'am.

They've also come here today, saying, they'll enforce this. Enforcement isn't the issue here. We've tried to run this, as best as we can, as a change debate, but we see that in any case, enforcement is still going to be a problem in a model. The fact is that there are different countries and there are different forms, Ladies and Gentlemen, so, **even if**, and we have this model here, enforcement is going to be an issue, and we accept that.

And thirdly they have come out saying we have to be accountable. Well, Ladies and Gentlemen, accountability doesn't exactly do wonders for the poor either. The fact is that, when we – when countries – when they pay bribes, generally to poor countries, which are the ones where corruption is allowed, generally to <u>social servants</u>, who <u>usually get paid less anyway</u>. So, this is paying the social servants what the government can't afford. So, we see that this is [*("On That Point, Sir" Paulina offers a POI – Tim ignores her)*] not hurting poor countries economy, which is good. [*(" Sir" Domingo offers a POI – Tim ignores him)*] Because the rich people have to spend money on the economy, which eventually gets shared around through the great rules of economy to the [*("On That Point, Sir." Valentina offers a POI – Tim looks at her, and accepts)*] I'll take you in one – actually, Yes.

Valentina Salvatierra: "Are you aware of the fact that most of the money doesn't get to the people – that it stays in the hands of a privledged few?"

Tim responds: "Yes, Ma'am, but the fact is that the privledged few don't just sit there – just sit there on the side of the road holding their money and going, "Wow, look at all of the money I've got," Ladies and Gentlemen. Rich people go out and they spend their money, on things that the poor people have created. Therefore what they spend it on benefits the poor [*Paulina looks amused at this answer, Domingo refuses to let it go by ... ("On That Point, Sir!" Domingo offers a POI – Tim ignores him)*] Then what the poor people have created suddenly becomes greater value. The poor people get the money. That's the way the economy works. The redistribution of wealth, Ladies and Gentlemen. (*"On That Point, Sir." Paulina offers a POI – Timrefuses.)]* No thank you, Ma'am.

I'm just gonna move on to this whole idea of not restricting sovereignty at all. They say that this is such an important principle that it stands alone. That's the basis of all international (*"Sir." Domingo softly offers a POI – Tim ignores him.)]* agreements, even if, something is wrong. They say that all the countries in the world think that corruption is wrong, which is not the case, Ladies and Gentlemen. **Even if** that was true, then what happens is that we should still allow the few countries to decide what they will do or not do. It's their own country. And they are allowed to make their own decisions and reach their own conclusions. It's the basis of all international law, Ladies and Gentlemen. And we see that if we start going and taking away this, we see that it hurts all – it hurts foreign relations as we view this. The whole Saudi Arabia example, if someone were to investigate, it wouldn't provide intel on terrorist attacks. These terrorists could be attacking the British, could be attacking the – uh – UK Ladies and Gentlemen. And they would not know, because they are **on their high horse**, running about, enforcing, what they view to be corruption. And as we have said, it fits nicely into the whole cultural imperialism thing, in the Middle Eastern (*"On That Point, Sir." Paulina offers a POI – Tim ignores her)]* countries, they practice "Bakshish". Bakshish is a cultural practice Ladies and Gentlemen. It's charity, payment to receive certain favors, and we see that this would be viewed as bribery in western countries. But the fact is that this simple (*"On That Point, Sir." Valentina offers a POI – Tim ignores her)]* practice is traditional and it's culturally expected. This is how business operates in these countries. It's not fair for us to go out there, imposing culture on other countries with which we deal – and it's unfair to their way of life. (Domingo whispers something to Valentina while Paulina... (*"On That Point, Sir." Paulina offers a POI – Tim accepts)]* Actually, Yes.

Paulina: "We have already told you that most countries do have corruption as something wrong and illegal. The only thing we're trying to do here is doing something that would be much easier to enforce...

Tim: "**I get your point**. There are countries that do have Bakshish as being legal. The fact is what some countries, and what we have seen, is that although there are exceptions, all countries do have slightly different perceptions about this point. It just shows that the case we have brought to you today, Ladies and Gentlemen, the fact is that every country has got slightly different views on what is corruption or what isn't. If you go out there, doing what they are doing, international agreement laws Ladies and Gentlemen, we think and we say that what is going to happen is that there are gonna be countries that miss out. And this is where cultural imperialism comes in, Ma'am.

So, **on to the next point**, about the whole restriction of business. This is also why bribery doesn't harm business. A popular belief over on that side (*Team Chile*). They say that, if we restrict business by saying that, "When a business is overseas, they still have to adhere to our rules, to what we view as being corruption or not, this puts certain restrictions on them. Look at –

if they are in a country that bribe – and they walk up to someone's house, with a bottle of wine, or a 25 thousand dollar boat, whatever happens, this is what we're speaking about – culture, they cannot do it because of us. And this makes it harder for them to make friends in the business industry, makes it (*ting, a bell sounds, indicating Tim has one more minute left in his speech – no more POIs can be asked in the final minute*) harder to culture, to make it in business. Because Ladies and Gentlemen, business is all about the little things, it's all about little relations we have with people, it's about, "I really like you – I wanna invest in your company", it's all about that, Ladies and Gentlemen. And we say these businesses are not constructed from laws which are in our country and even though in the other country that's expected that they do that Ladies and Gentlemen, this can be taken as <u>offensive</u> and it makes for certain difficult situations. (*Paulina whispers something to Valentina*) Look, a great example is the environment. (*Domingo stands up and leans over Paulina's shoulder to point something out to Valentina*)

The environment is something that most countries find important. But they still allow businesses to go to China and to adhere to the environmental standards. (*Domingo continues to confer with Valentina – finally sitting down after a few seconds more. As soon as he sits, Paulina turns to Valentina and whispers more information to her*)

The fact of the matter is, Ladies and Gentlemen, we have to respect the decisions that China has made. And every individual country has made Ladies and Gentlemen. We say, that **because of** the principle of respecting sovereignty, **because** it is unfair to impose our cultural imperialism, *(ting, the bell sounds, indicating Tim's time is up – he must finish his speech in the next ten seconds)* and **because** our businesses are going overseas *(ting-ting, indicating his time is finished)* and need to be able to adhere to those rules of those countries, to what is expected of them, we say, that **therefore**, <u>countries should not punish those who pay bribes to officials of other countries</u>. Thank You.

*** End of 3<sup>rd</sup> Proposition Speech

3nd Opposition Speaker: Valentina Salvatierra  (8 minutes)

(Valentina delivers her speech **standing behind the podium**, with a microphone.)

Valentina Salvatierra: "Crimes are crimes, where-ever they are committed. We must try to eliminate the supply side of bribery, to diminish it as a whole. And this is what we have tried to defend today. To move toward a world, where legality and transparency, and the rule of law, are enforced world-wide. What the Proposition (Team) wants is to actually take a huge step backwards because we are defending – eh - certain traditional cultures that by the way - **they have completely misunderstood.** And therefore, I can fairly confidently say, the main areas of dispute in this debate were, first of all, cultural imposition and whether it is occurring or not in this case. And second of all, transparency and rule of law versus other priorities which they identified such as, economic development and terrorist intelligence.

**Let me move on to the first area of dispute**. Is imposition of values really occurring here and how harmful, really, is this supposed imposition of values? First of all, *(ting, the bell sounds, indicating one minute has gone by – POIs can now be asked)* in many countries it's not that [*("Ma'am".) A POI is offered by Nicholas – and ignored – by Valentina- Nicholas continues to stand)*] corruption is legal, it's that these countries are vulnerable countries that do not have the (*Valentina motions for Nicholas to sit down*) sovereignty at this moment to enforce the laws that they themselves have set in place.

Or they do not have the political will to pursue the corrupt officials. However, this doesn't mean that this isn't a crime there. [*("Ma'am". Tim Robinson offers a POI – Valentina ignores him – he remains standing)*] And if it isn't being punished there, it's perfectly valid for the crime to be punished elsewhere because it's still a crime, as I stated previously. No thank you. (*She motions for Tim to sit down*)

**Furthermore, I would like to** clear up your concept of gift-giving. Many of these bribes are based on individual greed and not on customs. You spoke of gift-giving and how it was used in relationships between people. Well, I'd like to clear that up. In China – China is a country that is big on gift-giving. This is used to strengthen, trust, caring [(*"Ma'am". Nicholas Orr offers a POI – Valentina motions for him to sit down)*] reciprocity and commitment.

However, gift-giving is not the same as bribery because gift-giving is done between people who have some sort of personal relationship and bribery is done only on [(*"But Ma'am". Nicholas offers a POI – Valentina motions for him to sit down)*] economic business related things.  In these examples, other values must reign supreme over respecting obsolete traditions.   The value of fair competition must overcome cultural tradition.   [(*" Point Of Information, Ma'am". James Penn offers a POI – Valentina motions for him to sit down)*] We can't allow cultural traditions to get us stuck in a culture of mediocrity because that is what it is. Because we are not promoting values that actually encourage [(*" Point Of Information, Ma'am". Tim Robinson offers a POI – Valentina ignores him)*]   fair competition  –  that  help  the consumers, that help the whole economy.   We are defending traditions just because they are traditions?   Frankly, if traditions are harmful, we must leave them behind.   **Even if** it were an Equatorial Guinean tradition to accept gifts, **it's not valid to argue that** just because it's a tradition, it justifies that – the dictator that currently rules in that country, is making huge profits from his dealings with Exxon Oil Company, while 70% of his people live in poverty.  That's not justified by saying that it's a cultural tradition [(*" But Ma'am". James Penn offers a POI – Valentina accepts the POI – I Will Now Take Your Point)*]

James Penn: "Can you establish – can you tell us how –  when a dictator takes the money, it actually – from a company – it actually takes away money from the citizens?

Valentina:  "It takes away money from the citizens because this company has actually run the oil business that it establishes there, inefficiently,   and   therefore   it   hasn't   provided   economic development the way a more efficient company would.  Why is it still there?  Because it's paying bribes to the dictator that rules that country.  Does that seem fair to you?  Does it seem fair to you that simply because some companies have more money to pay bribes, [(*" But Ma'am". James Penn offers another POI – Valentina motions for him to sit down saying – "No thank you".)*] They are getting unfair advantage over companies that perhaps do the job better?  That's what we're aiming at.

***Dear Reader – James Penn asked Paulina a question which she did not answer: "How does the dictator taking bribes mean taking money away from the citizens?" Her answer about efficiency and fairness does not show a <u>reasonable link</u>, a connection, between bribe money going in the dictator's pocket and money being taken away from the people. However, her answer was a rhetorical one – She appealed to the <u>emotion</u> (*Pathos*) of her audience and the judges – most people would agree with her on an <u>emotional level</u> – that no, <u>it's not fair</u> for the dictator to take bribes while 70% of his people lives in poverty. However, that was not the question that James asked her. She avoided answering the difficult question by picking an issue that she could win – fairness. Nonetheless, on a logical level (*Logos*) Valentina's answer was glaringly <u>deficient</u>. It was a non-answer. What can James do? He can only point out - in his team's next speech - that she failed to answer the question properly. If he doesn't, Valentina will have avoided negative consequences to once again, another <u>excellent question</u> from James Penn.

How about it Dear Reader – How Would You Answer James Penn's question?***

Valentina continues: "You spoke about the economy, so [(" *Point Of Information". James Penn offers a POI – Valentina motions for him to sit down)*] [(" *But Ma'am". Nicholas Orr offers a POI – Valentina motions for him to sit down)*] No thank you. - *(unintelligible)* cultural values is not an absolute value. **And this is where I move on to** the <u>second area</u> of <u>dispute.</u> <u>Transparency and the rule of law versus other priorities.</u> (** Here we see Valentina has labelled the disputed area for the judges convenience – making it easy to follow her speech) <u>I'd like to point out</u> that the Proposition (Team) has set us up in a **false dichotomy** here [(*"But Ma'am".Nicholas Orr offers a POI – Valentina motions for him to sit down – and reprimands him, saying: "No thank you. Let me finish.")*] <u>They have said</u> that for instance, we wouldn't have gotten terrorist information, we wouldn't have gotten economic deals, <u>if we didn't engage in bribery.</u> **However**, this is based on certain **false facts**, because we can still get the deals, we can still make business. <u>One thing does</u>

not eliminate the other. In fact, economic development and transparency go hand in hand. Let me **explain** to you **why**. You spoke about how prohibiting bribery would hurt the "masses" (*Valentina uses air quotation marks as she says the word – masses*). Actually, allowing masses hurts the masses. **Because** the countries that take bribes are undeveloped countries. Undeveloped countries get most of their jobs from small and medium companies. And small and medium companies are precisely the ones that are hurt most by foreign bribery. **Why**? [(*"Ma'am". Nicholas Orr offers a POI – Valentina motions for him to sit down*)] Because they can't compete with – uh – a huge multinational that is paying bribes to win the adjudications that the government puts forth? **So, is that fair**? [(*"Point Of Information". James Penn vigorously attempts to offer a POI –his voice dripping with indignation - Valentina has argued without any sources, without factual evidence or examples to support her position – and she again appeals to emotion,"Is That Fair" – Valentina ignores James – He remains standing*)] Does it help the economy? It does not help the economy. **Because it hurts** the businesses that are actually the vast majority in these developing countries. Yes Sir, I Will Take Your Question.

James Penn: "Ma'am, is it worth the lives of innocent British people, simply to enforce corruption around the world?"

\*\*\* Valentina pauses to think carefully. She knows that she has been making arguments <u>without giving evidence</u>, <u>without naming sources</u>, and <u>appealing</u> to the <u>emotion</u> of her audience and the judges. This is called **"throwing the kitchen sink"** at your opponent. It means that **even if** some of your arguments aren't very good, your opponent still has to take the time to deal with them – and at this late stage of the debate – Team NZ is running out of time. With so many potential openings given to him, James shows his brilliance as a debater.

Rather than ask a question on a minor point – he has focused his question on an area that could cause tremendous damage to Team Chile – that the COST of following their counter-plan could potentially result in the **loss of human life** – and **death** is **irreversible**. Valentina must answer this question very carefully – it is meant to change the outcome of the debate if she gives the wrong answer.\*\*\*

Valentina responds: "This takes me to something that I had wanted to point out before. Thank you for bringing that up again. Because, they seem to have argued, from the beginning, and throughout the whole case, on merely one example. Disregarding the many examples of corruption that exists in the world. And this is clearly not a strong line of argument for the Proposition."

\*\*\* Valentina simply avoided the question – giving no answer at all - while reprimanding the Proposition team (NZ) for the way they chose to conduct the debate. So, Dear Reader – here's my challenge for you: Imagine you are Team New Zealand. You have only one ( 1 ) speech left – a 4 minute summary speech. How do you make the judges and audience aware that Valentina has avoided answering both questions that she was asked? What do you say – and how do you say it? Also, how do you make the judges and audience aware that her arguments in the latter part of her speech were not based on evidence, no sources were named, and she repeatedly appealed to their **emotion** rather than their **intellect**, their reasoning ability? What do you say – and how do you say it?\*\*\*

Valentina continues: "Furthermore, they spoke about the jobs of public servants [(*"But Ma'am". Nicholas Orr offers a POI – Valentina motions for him to sit down)*] No thank you. And about how their priorities could not – were not compatible with transparency. **Once again**, they have put **us** before a **false dichotomy**. Insofar as corruption hurts the whole developing countries economy, it's also hurting the public officials themselves. Insofar as a country doesn't develop as a whole, the hope of the public officials of getting decent salaries is further diminished. They are trapped in a self-perpetuating cycle where they are forced to accept bribes, and it perpetuates their countries economic lack of development [(*"Ma'am". James Penn offers a POI – Valentina ignores him)*] Therefore they are forced to receive more bribes. **Is this logical**? **Is this fair**? **Should this be allowed to continue**? The answer clearly is **No!** (*No thank you. She motions for James to sit down.*) It's **absurd** to say that lack of transparency can ultimately help a country with its economy. It simply perpetuates a culture where the best services – where the best products and the best services aren't prioritised. Where, what is actually prioritised is – Who bids the most? [(*"But Ma'am". Nicholas Orr offers a POI – Valentina motions for him to sit down)*] - - for the business. **That's simply not valid**. Corruption siphons away funds from areas that are more prior – it diminishes economic development – It cannot be – (*ting, the bell sounds, Valentina has one more minute to speak*) and don't like the Proposition (Team) would like to defend. **In fact**, their argument about sovereignty. Bribing officials gradually buys you international sovereignty. **How's that, for a position Ladies and Gentlemen**? So, the whole Proposition case has been built entirely on one example – a rich country (UK) bribing another rich country (Saudi Arabia). We would like to propose to you – we would like to mention to you that – the most – that the most corrupt countries, according to all countries indexes (?) are also very poor countries – vulnerable countries. They are not comparable to the case that they used to base their whole argument on. And it's no coincidence – this fact that many poor countries are very corrupt countries. Let's keep the current legislation, and try to better enforce it – try to reach more international agreement. Let's not allow difficulties in enforcement, or agreeing on what a bribe is Ladies and Gentlemen – that doesn't require a meeting. (*ting-ting, the bell sounds, indicating Valentina's time is up, she must finish in the next 10 seconds*) <u>Let's</u> not allow these to **<u>deter us</u>** from trying. And **<u>let's</u> oppose this defeatist motion**. Thank You.

\*\*\*

End of 3<sup>rd</sup> Opposition Speaker's Speech

\*\*\*Dear Reader, what happened?  Both speeches seemed to be going over everything that had already been dealt with in the first two speeches.  Why not wait until the final summary speech to do this?

Wouldn't that be the best time to summarise what had already been said?    Besides, won't the judges find it boring to hear everything all over again?

The answer is, No.  This speech, the 3<sup>rd</sup> Speech, is the most important speech in the whole debate.  Why?  You identify what the major areas of dispute were.

You rebut all the major arguments of the other team – you rebuild all of your team's major arguments.

You inform the judges if the other team did not deal with one of your arguments.  This is called, a "**dropped argument**".

You look at all the arguments and clearly show that you have won the arguments that are necessary for the judges to determine that your team is the winner.

In the 3<sup>rd</sup> speeches between Team NZ and Team Chile , Team Chile convinced all **<u>NINE</u>** (9) judges that they should be judged the winner.  That was an amazing achievement, almost unheard of to be so superior to a very skilled team like Team New Zealand. There can be no doubt that NZ were a great team, in their own right.

WSDC-Style – Debate Order & Speaker Roles

| 1st Proposition – New Zealand (James) | 1st Opposition – Chile (Domingo) |
|---|---|
| Opening (to get audience attention)<br>Define the motion<br>Signpost Speech Structure<br>3 Arguments<br>Summary | Opening (to get audience attention)<br>Signpost Speech Structure<br>Rebuttal of all 1st Prop Arguments<br>3 Arguments<br>Summary |
| 2nd Proposition – (Nicholas)<br>Opening ( audience attention)<br>Rebuttal of all 1st Opp Arguments<br>Rebuild<br>2 New Arguments<br>Summary | 2nd Opposition – (Paulina)<br>Opening ( audience attention)<br>Rebuttal of all 2nd Prop Arguments<br>Rebuild<br>2 New Arguments<br>Summary |
| 3rd Proposition – (Tim)<br>Opening (to get audience attention)<br>Signpost Speech Structure:<br>Rebuttal of <u>most important</u> Arguments by 1st & 2nd Opp<br>Rebuild Arguments dealt with by Opp<br>Restate Arguments not dealt with by Opp<br>Summary | 3rd Opposition – (Valentina)<br>Opening (to get audience attention)<br>Signpost Speech Structure:<br>Rebuttal of <u>most important</u> Arguments by 1st & 2nd Prop<br>Rebuild Arguments dealt with by Prop<br>Restate Arguments not dealt with by Prop<br>Summary |
| 4th Proposition – Reply speech – (James)<br>(Given **after** the Opposition summary)<br>Given by 1st Prop or 2nd Prop Speaker<br>Opening<br>Theme 1<br>Theme 2<br>Theme 3 | 4th Opposition – Reply Speech (Paulina)<br>(Given **before** the Proposition Summary)<br>Given by 1st Opp or 2nd Opp Speaker<br>Opening<br>Theme 1<br>Theme 2<br>Theme 3 |

4<sup>th</sup> Opp Reply Speaker: Paulina Valenzuela (4 minutes- No POIs – Reverse Order)

Paulina Valenzuela: "Ladies and Gentlemen, today I'm going to close the case and reply to what the Proposition has said about corruption here. To do this, we want to analyse three (3) main principles. First: Does bribery harm the economy? Second: Are international relationships possible without bribery? And third: It is justified to impose cultural imperialism? And the answers to these questions are: **Yes, Yes, and Yes**. Why, you might ask?

First of all, does bribery harm the economy? Here the Proposition (Team) has done a thing that is **unbelievable**. They have said that actually bribery helps the economy. They have said that when a leader receives a bribe, he would go to the markets of his city and spend them on things done by the poor so that the poor would be happy and thus their economy will grow. This is totally **ridiculous**. Totally utopic. I mean, if it was like that, the ten most corrupted countries of the world wouldn't be ten of the most poor. If it was like that, the Guinean dictator wouldn't have all his money under Riggs Bank, **would he**? So, these are **ridiculous**. Bribery harms the economy, **because** it makes market competition

120

impossible. **Because** it decreases the value of giving out a good product and it increases the value of giving out a good bribe. So, it harms the economy? Yes, it does. **And this point was clearly won** by the Opposition (Team).

<u>Now</u>, are international relationships possible without bribery? The Proposition (Team) has here too almost said the only way countries can interact is by bribing each other. And we think this is not only **ridiculous**, but **offensive**. Many countries don't bribe each other. **My** country (*proudly and passionately spoken by Paulina with extra emphasis on the word "my"*) for example, is not corrupted, does not appear on the most corrupted countries of the world, and I think that it's **offensive** to say, that these countries that don't bribe each other, are almost, cut out of the world. I mean, this doesn't mean that because you don't bribe each other, you can't deal with other countries. The only thing you would be doing here, Ladies and Gentlemen, is making that deal fair. Is making that deal transparent. And this is good. So, this is why this point was won by the Opposition (Team) too.

<u>And third</u>: It is justified to impose cultural imperialism, as they have insisted to call, Yes, it is. But what cultural imperialism? Not the imposal of western culture, the imposal of the culture of transparency. This culture is shared on all around the world. And the only thing we want to do here, is impose that, the culture that being transparent is better than being corrupt. The culture, that when you transparent, you are much more successful. Bribery creates an awful market. (*ting, the bell sounds; Paulina has one minute left in her speech*) Creates awful opportunities, and creates unfair differences between countries. And we have proved this to you throughout the debate. What the Proposition (Team) has continuously trying to do, saying that corruption is not important, and this is certainly not true. Corruption affects every – every aspect of our daily lives. And this is why we should have force against it. And it is possible Ladies and Gentlemen. And we dearly believe this. By the way, the Dictator of Guinea sends you his kind greetings from his cruiser in the Arabian Gulf. Thank you very much.

*** End of 4th Opposition Reply Speech

4<sup>th</sup> Prop Reply Speaker: James Penn (4 minutes- No POIs – Final Speech)

James Penn: "To quote the third speaker from Team Chile: "Crime's are crimes, wherever they're done". What we're here debating today, Ladies and Gentlemen, is that paying bribes to foreign officials should not be a crime. Now Ladies and Gentlemen, we can get our table to tap loudly on the desk, if you want, but the fact of the matter is, we don't need to, because we have justification for our arguments.

Now today, I'm gonna be looking at how this debate went, in three key areas: **Firstly**, I'm gonna look at this rather surprising counter-model that was brought out by Team Chile. **Then** I'm gonna move on to sovereignty and cultural imperialism, and **then** I'm gonna move on to the question: Does it have economic harms?

So this counter-model that we heard from Team Chile today. They talked about an international agreement on stamping out bribes. Ladies and Gentlemen, we've clearly established that some cultures, many cultures, don't have the same ideals in terms of bribes, as other cultures. And because of this, we say that an international agreement, is never gonna be reached. Then they talked about in their model, it's only gonna be in the form of monetary exchanges, Ladies and Gentlemen, we all know that I can give someone a gift worth 25 thousand dollars and say, "Give me something in return". It doesn't have to be a personal – um – exchange. So, we also think that – um – if it includes gifts, people would just stop – I mean if it excludes gifts – uh – in their counter-model – people would just stop giving gifts more than monetary exchanges anyway.

So on to the big issue of sovereignty and cultural imperialism. Now, we've established that different countries have very different cultural traditions. And that there are countries that have processes which may be viewed by other countries as bribes. Ladies and Gentlemen, we must protect these values. We must protect these cultural views. It is morally wrong, it is morally reprehensible to stop imposing one country's – um - moral views on another. **We didn't really get a response to this** – the response they gave is kinda shying away – is that bribes deny sovereignty for other countries. **We ask you today Ladies and Gentlemen, which is more important**: Numerous entire state's sovereignty or a few companies' sovereignty? Ladies and Gentlemen, here on Side Proposition, we advocate for the States. And we advocate for the people's sovereignty to be maintained.

Now, another point they didn't really address, actually throughout this debate, and we think it's one that the debate is rather centered around in terms of the context, is the fact that if you start to punish bribes, from individuals to foreign officials, then you start to – um - get hindrance to foreign relations. (*ting, the bell sounds; James Penn has one more minute left*) We think that it's very essential today, in today's debate.

Now, quickly on to the question: Does it have economic harms? They talked about Guinea - - and they didn't really establish how bribes are made by the whole country - - **We accept** that the Guinea leader pockets the money, but did that mean that any money was taken away from the citizens? We say No. Their response, when I actually brought it up in a POI, they said that it keeps companies from running efficiently. This may be a common point of view, but it is rather **short-sighted**, Ladies and Gentlemen. That is every company's incentive to be run at the most efficient form. If they charge astronomical prices, then they won't get people buying their products or services. So we think that response – that they run inefficiently, is rather **short-sighted**. So, Ladies and Gentlemen, because – um – punishing individuals who pay bribes to foreign officials of other countries, - um – uh – is a demonstration of cultural imperialism (*ting-ting, James Penn has run out of time – he must finish his speech in ten seconds*) because their counter-model just doesn't stack up, and because it doesn't have any economical harms, **we are proud to propose**."

\***The Debate Ends

**References**

Snider, Alfred. (2008). The code of the debater: Introduction to policy debating. New York: International Debate Education Association.

Wooden, John. (2009). Coach Wooden's leadership game plan for success: 12 lessons for extraordinary performance and personal excellence. New York: McGraw-Hill.

# Chapter 13

## Debating In the Classroom

*"Rhetoric is the art of persuading the minds of men."* ~ Plato

By the end of November, 2008, my elementary class of twenty-five (25) 6th-grade boys had finished their textbook and taken the final exams for the 2008 school year. Every student had passed and would be going on to 7th grade. But there were still three more weeks of school left! What could be done to fill the time productively? The purpose of this first chapter is to share with the reader(s) why and how debate was used to resolve this common problem that teachers face.

### Why debates?

There were two main reasons. First, various debate activities had been used in the past as a class speaking activity. One favourite is the "Balloon Debate". In this activity, a group of four to eight students is formed. Each student chooses to be a famous person who is in a balloon that is rapidly losing altitude.

The group can only be saved if one person sacrifices themself by jumping overboard. To decide who must jump, each student must give reasons why they should stay in the balloon. The teacher and/or the class (by voting) then decides who has made the least persuasive argument. That person must jump. This process continues until there is only one person left in the balloon, who lands safely, winning the debate.

The second, and most significant, reason for using debates with this class of sixth graders was because of a movie, "The Great Debaters" (2007). It was directed by Denzel Washington. In it

Denzel also plays the role of Melvin Tollson, coach of the undefeated Wiley College Debate Team of 1935.

At the beginning of the movie there is a simple yet powerful scene. Denzel is explaining his philosophy about debating. The room is full of nervous students who are trying out for the debate team:

Denzel: "Debate is combat. Your weapons are words. In a debate there is a resolution. One team, called the affirmative team, argues for the resolution.

The other team, called the negative team, argues against the resolution."

That explanation - - clear and direct - - not only clarifies but also inspires. Students eagerly accepted the inherent challenge to "use words as weapons."

## Benefits of debating

One major benefit of debating in teams is the collaboration among team members. This social interaction is considered essential by social interactionist theorists, such as Tomasello (2003), Tomasello, Kruger, and Ratner (1993) and Vygotsky (1962, 1978), who state that learning involves the internalization of social interaction processes.

Additionally, other benefits have been claimed. At the 2006 JALT Hokkaido Language Conference a presentation entitled, "*Teaching Debate in the EFL Classroom*", was given by Manning and Nakamura. They have developed a debate course for high school EFL students in Japan. According to Manning and Nakamura:

• Debating ability is a valuable skill.

• Debate utilizes useful English.

• It is a unique way to teach grammar.

• It develops critical thinking skills.

• It introduces global issues.

• It develops research skills.

Let's take a closer look at their ideas, in a general manner. First of all, there can be little doubt that debating is a valuable skill. If we are able to become skilled at presenting our opinions to others, the possible benefits to be gained are almost unlimited. To name only a few: increased self-confidence, making criteria-based decisions, public speaking, and positive interpersonal relationships all come quickly to mind as areas which may be positively affected by gaining the ability to debate.

Secondly, in terms of learning a language, regardless of whether it is a first, second, or foreign language, to participate successfully requires that participants increase their vocabulary. Further, they must also learn to put the vocabulary into expressive forms which can be adapted to a wide variety of speaking situations. In this sense, time spent on debate is well invested.

Thirdly, grammar is being taught coincidentally, embedded into the language that is being used. Grammar is always present, yet the focus is not on learning a particular grammatical item. The focus is on the effective use of English. Therefore, grammar is learned that is needed to accomplish this comunicative goal. This can be thought of as learning grammar naturally, in order to express oneself in a meaningful way that is persuasion oriented.

Fourthly, critical thinking is at the heart of debate. It promotes independent thought processes which seek to understand by examining issues from the standpoint of the evidence that supports a particular position. If the logic and evidence is clear and unequivocal, critical thinking will most likely lead the student to accept a particular position.

On the other hand, if the evidence is not consistent, or is in some way contradictory, the student will most likely reject the position which has been adopted. This way of thinking makes people capable of living in a world that continuously seeks to persuade them to take one decision or another: buying a product, health care, education, automobile, home, vacation, etc.

Fifthly, debating is an excellent platform from which to consider global issues. Nowadays, we live in a globalised world that is interconnected and interdependent. What happens in one part of the world has an almost immediate effect, in one way or another, in another part of the world.

The problems the world is facing are increasingly of such magnitude that solutions require bringing together the best minds, knowledge, skills and abilities of people from a wide diversity of backgrounds in all countries. This requires an awareness of global issues. Debating lends itself well to the examination and discussion of these topics that have global significance.

Finally, research skills are necessary if one is to consider debate topics in any depth. For example, in a debate about using animals for sport and entertainment, it is safe to say that most people do not think that animals should be abused or mistreated. Since this happens in many instances, most inexperienced debaters would not consider doing research.

This would be a fatal mistake, because the opposing team would present a wide variety of factual, statistical, and first-person evidence that would be convincing. To avoid such an outcome, effective research must be undertaken. In sum, to debate effectively, an opinion is not enough. Evidence gained from research must be used to provide clear and compelling support for a particular position.

## Why debate?

Next, let's turn to Dr. Alfred Snider, Director of the World Debate Institute at the University of Vermont. He lists six answers to the question, "Why debate?" (Snider, 1999, p.5). They are:

• Debating is fun.

• Debating is a sport of the mind and voice.

• Debating is controlled by you.

• Debating creates the skills you need for success in life.

• Debate can give you the power to change things.

• Debating is not just for "geeks" or "nerds".

Dr. Snider's six reasons present universal truths. Participating in a debate is a way to have good, clean fun. It is the ideas we debate, not the people. It is truth we seek, not manipulation. Matching wits with friends is without a doubt fun for debaters.

Further, it is not enough to use your mind. Logic is necessary, yes, but the voice must be used also. An idea that remains in your mind, and is never voiced, is not helpful to anyone. How do we give voice to our thoughts in such a way that others will pay attention to what we have to say? Debating gives valuable practice in acquiring this essential skill of speaking well in public.

The debater controls the debate. The development of the debate responds to the way that the debaters attempt to prove their ideas. Whether one seeks to employ logic, emotion, or credibility (in the Greek: *Logos*, *Pathos*, *Ethos*) or some combination of all these elements of persuasive speech, depends entirely on the strengths and weaknesses of each debater individually, and likewise on the strengths and weaknesses of the team collectively. Let me give an example:

If your team is made up of all boys, it can argue very convincingly for sports in school, based on personal experience. Yet this same team would not be able to argue convincingly to ban beauty contests, as the element of personal experience is not available to them. They would have to seek other sources who are capable of speaking authoritatively on this topic. Hence, the control of the debate is defined by the participants themselves, based on the strategy they choose to use for the debate.

Are debating skills only for academic purposes, useful only in school, without any real world use later in life? The answer is "No". There is an incredibly long list of successful people who participated in debate when they were young. To name only a few:

• Former UN Secretary General **Kofi Annan** competed in the early 60's for Macalester College in St. Paul, Minnesota.

• South African President **Nelson Mandela** debated in college.

• Former British Prime Minister **Margaret Thatcher** competed in debate.

• Former British Prime Minister **John Major** competed in debate.

• President **Lyndon Baines Johnson** taught high school debate.

• John F. Kennedy's speech writer and executive assistant **Ted Sorenson**, debated in high school and college.

• **Oprah Winfrey** competed in debate in high school.

• **Tom Brokaw** debated at South Dakota State.

• In his book, *Confessions*, **St. Augustine** writes, "from age 18 to 35, I was a teacher of public speaking."

• In addition to the many celebrated debates of his public career, **Malcolm X** debated teams from Harvard, Yale, and other New England colleges as part of the Norfolk Prison (Massachusetts) debating program. Read more about it in "*'I Was Gone on Debating': Malcolm X's Prison Debates and Public Confrontations*", by Robert Branham, debate coach at Bates College, published in **Argumentation and Advocacy**, v. 31, Winter, 1995.

• Cicero, Demosthenes, Plato, Socrates, and Aristotle.

Cicero's *"De Oratore"*, now at the **British Museum**.

## Oratory is attractive but difficult http://bit.ly/1eAC7FF

Cicero claims that in Athens, "where the supreme power of oratory was both invented and perfected," no other art study has a more vigorous life than the art of speaking.

After first trying rhetoric without training or rules, using only natural skill, young orators listened and learned from Greek orators and teachers, and soon were much more enthusiastic for eloquence.

Young orators learned, through practice, the importance of variety and frequency of speech. In the end, orators were awarded with popularity, wealth, and reputation.

But Cicero warns that oratory fits into more arts and areas of study than people might think. This is the reason why this particular subject is such a difficult one to pursue. Students of oratory must have a knowledge of many matters to have successful rhetoric. They must also form a certain style through word choice and arrangement. Students must also learn to understand human emotion so as to appeal to their audience.

This means that the student must, through his style, bring in humor and charm—as well as the readiness to deliver and respond to an attack.

Moreover, a student must have a significant capacity for memory—they must remember complete histories of the past, as well as of the law.

Cicero reminds us of another difficult skill required for a good orator: a speaker must deliver with control—using gestures, playing and expressing with features, and changing the intonation of the voice.

In summary, oratory is a combination of many things, and to succeed in maintaining all of these qualities is a great achievement.

Amazon reviewer George R. Dekle: http://amzn.to/18xOpwX

"This is a review of "De Oratore" books I-II and "De Oratore" book III in the Loeb Classical Library. Marcus Tullius Cicero wrote much on many subjects, and some of his private correspondence also survives. He did his best writing in the field of rhetoric. Although he was not an original thinker on the subject of rhetoric, "De Oratore" shows him to have had an encyclopedic practical knowledge of oratory in general and criminal trial advocacy in particular.

Cicero wrote "De Oratore" as a dialog among some of the preeminent orators of the era immediately preceding Cicero's time. The occasion is a holiday at a country villa, and the characters discuss all facets of oratory, ceremonial, judicial, and deliberative. They devote most of the discussion to judicial oratory, and their discussion reveals the trial of a Roman lawsuit to be somewhat analogous to the trial of a modern lawsuit. You have to piece it together from stray references to procedure scattered throughout the work, but it appears that a Roman trial consisted of opening statements, the taking of evidence, and final arguments. Modern trial advocacy manuals devote most of their attention to the taking of evidence, but Cicero dismisses the mechanics of presenting evidence as relatively unimportant compared to the mechanics of presenting argument.

"De Oratore" is divided into three books. The first speaks of the qualities of the orator; the second of judicial oratory, and the third of ceremonial and deliberative oratory. The modern trial lawyer would find the second book most interesting and most enlightening. A lot about trial advocacy has changed since Cicero's day (e.g. no more testimony taken under torture), but a lot hasn't.

Trial lawyers cannot congregate without swapping "war stories," and Cicero's characters are no exception. They pepper their discussion with references to courtroom incidents which have such verisimilitude that they could have happened last week instead of 2,000 years ago. I have no doubt that Cicero, had he lived today, would have made a formidable trial lawyer."

## Are there any drawbacks to debating?

Yes! There can be arguments, shouting, insults, even physical attacks if a debate is not conducted in a respectful manner. It is therefore essential to ensure that debaters are taught to "disagree agreeably". Dr. Snider lists an excellent, "Code of the Debater" (Snider, 1999, p.13) in his book. Three rules of his Code of Conduct were taught:

1. I will respect the rights of others to freedom of speech.

2. I will respect my partners, opponents, judges and coaches.

3. I will be a generous winner and a gracious loser.

## How was debating taught to sixth-grade students?

First, the class was informed that for the final three weeks they would be debating. The students were then divided into six mixed-ability teams of four students each. One of the best students was selected to be my "Assistant Coach".

Next, the meanings of the terms: *resolution, affirmative team*, and *negative team* were explained. Turn-taking was explained: One member of the affirmative team speaks first, then one from the negative team. This continues until everyone has spoken.

After that, the speaking roles of the four team members were explained. The first speaker on each team is the Captain. This person introduces their teammates and outlines the main arguments their team will make. The second and third speaker for each team, in turn, presents their argument for, or against, the resolution.

The final speaker for each team summarises the arguments their team has made. It must be noted that each speaker briefly *refutes* (finds fault with) the previous speaker's arguments. Additionally, one question from the opposing team had to be answered by the second and third speaker on each team.

The "winner" is the team that has scored highest in three categories: **teamwork** (strategy), **content** (argument) and **delivery** (how well the speech was made). The students are judged on a scale of 1 – 10 in each category with 30 points being a perfect score.

The judge's decision is final. After announcing the winner, the judge briefly explains the debate scoring and offers constructive criticism to both teams. Respectful discussion, including questions and opinions, are allowed by both teams.

This kind of immediate, two-way, post-debate feedback is essential because it helps students to improve their performance as debaters.

As a fun, motivational activity, the class copied and memorized the following, "Debater's Creed" from the movie, "The Great Debaters":

Denzel: "Who is the judge?"

Debaters: "God is the judge."

Denzel: "Why is God the judge?"

Debaters: "Because God decides who's right or wrong, not my opponent."

Denzel: "Who's your opponent?"

Debaters: "My opponent doesn't exist."

Denzel: "Why does your opponent not exist?"

Debaters: "Because our opponent is a voice dissenting from the truth I speak."

Denzel: "Speak the truth."

Debaters: "Speak the truth."

## Final preparation

In the next class the students reviewed what they had learned in the previous class. After that, each team captain introduced his teammates. Next, each team said the Debater's Creed. This was done in order; one team after the other rather than as a class. The Assistant Coach circulated from team to team and prompted students who needed help.

After that, all teams were given the same debate resolution: Resolved – "Spiderman is better than Superman". Working together, each team now had to decide what their arguments were going to be and in what order they would speak. The author and the Assistant Coach circulated, helping with vocabulary and grammar. At the end of the class the debate pairings/matches were agreed upon for the next class.

## The debates

It was decided that all speeches would last one minute. The Assistant Coach was the timekeeper. This author was both the Debate Chairperson and Judge. Each team debated on a resolution twice; once as the affirmative team and once as the negative team. After that the resolution was changed. While two teams were debating, the other four teams were the audience. The students debated the following resolutions:

Spiderman is better than Superman.
School uniforms are not necessary.
Students should not have to take tests.
Fast food restaurants should be banned.

## CONCLUSION

To sum up, the debates were lively and fun with all students participating. Debating was easily taught and quickly learned. Students used grammar and vocabulary they had learned during the year. This recycling helped them revise and consolidate their previous learning. They worked collaboratively and got practice in public speaking. Critical thinking skills were used to develop and refute arguments. Debating proved to be an enjoyable way to productively finish the year for the students. Finally, I recommend debating for all teachers, since it can be easily adapted to almost any teaching context.

## WORKS CITED
Baker, T. J. (2012): Teaching Debate in Chile. Lexington, Ky: CreateSpace Publishing House. http://bit.ly/159qVvp

Manning, M. & Nakamura, T. (2006). Teaching Debate in the EFL Classroom.

Snider, A. (1999). The code of the debater: Introduction to the way of reason. USA. Sponsored by the Open Society Institute, the World Debate Institute and the University of Vermont.

Tomasello, M. (2003). The key is social cognition. In *Language in mind; advances in the study of language and thought*. ed. D. Gentner and S. Goldin-Meadow.

Tomasello, M., Kruger, A. C., and Ratner, H. H. (1993). Cultural learning. *Behavioral and Brain Sciences*, 16, 495–552.

Vygotsky, L. (1962). Thought and language. Cambridge, MA: MIT Press. (Original work published 1934.)

_____ (1978). Mind in society: The development of higher psychological processes. ed. M. Cole. Cambridge, MA: Harvard University Press.

Washington, Denzel. (2007). The Great Debaters. Harpo Films.

# Chapter 14

Aristotle: "*Rhetoric may be defined as the faculty of observing, in any given case, the available means of persuasion.*"
["Rhetoric" BK I, Ch. 2. 1355b lines 26 - 27]

You just found out you're going to coach your school debate team. You're thrilled, right? Well, if you're like most debate coaches I have met, you got the job by being told you were going to be the debate coach. Non-negotiable. Sound familiar, huh?

OK, you're the coach of the debate team. You can't get out of it, so now what? Well, first of all, you need a team. You have to recruit some debaters.

What? How did I recruit debaters? In my case, I promised them an extra week of winter vacation. No, not really, I'm just kidding.

Here's some ideas, taken from an imaginative dialog:

Me: Remember what happened to you? You were told that you were the coach. So tell the students they are on your team.

You: What? That won't work!

Me: Hmm. Worked fine for me. But maybe that won't work for you. Alright, beg.

You: Beg?

Me: Beg. I'm serious. Beg the students to come to a tryout.

You: What? That won't work either. Nobody will come!

Me: I understand your dilemma. Hmm, how about this: **Be Honest**. Tell the students that debating requires long hours of practice. Tell them there is lots of research they have to do. Tell them debating is difficult, and all you can guarantee them is lots of long hours perfecting their debating skills.

You: What? Are you serious?

Me: Yes.

You: Do I have any other options?

Me: How about a movie? The most inspiring debating movie I can suggest is *"The Great Debaters"*, starring Denzell Washington. After they watch that movie, they will want to go out and debate somebody, anybody. Trust me, it is truly amaaaaaaaaazing!

To sum up, your first step in being a debate coach is to recruit a team. As a matter of fact, it's the most important thing you do. Recruit a team. Any way that you can, recruit a team.

Why?

Because a debate coach without a team is not a debate coach.

What if you have a team, now what? Watch these videos: http://bit.ly/Kja3rO

**Debate Delivers Dreams:**
**http://bit.ly/MJkSqd**

  **\*\***

**More Reasons Why Teaching Debate is A Very Good Idea**

Teaching debate, in Chile, or anywhere else in the world, is clearly a worthwhile endeavour. The purpose of this additional bit of encouragement for the debate coach is to share with you, the reader, my absolute certainty about the value of debate. I will give only three reasons, as I value your time. However, it must be said that there are many more than three (3) reasons why teaching debate is a good idea.

Firstly, the skills of debate will help you to solve disagreements peacefully. Thus, conflict is avoided. By conflict, I mean outright violence, whether physical or verbal. For example, let me mention the Arab-Israeli conflict. On an almost daily basis, the world news reports of some new fighting, some new bloodshed, some new atrocity.

Debating, in my view, is a more peaceful alternative. In a civilized world, regardless of all evidence to the contrary, it is possible to resolve disagreements through peaceful means. Even if the only thing you can do, is agree to disagree, debating is more productive (and life-preserving) than aggression.

Secondly, I want to emphasize that debating develops critical thinking. It teaches participants how to think for themselves. In a debate, for instance, you must listen carefully to the assertions of the opposite team. Any unsupported information that is relevant to the debate will be challenged.

You ask, for example, "Who is your expert opinion from? What is the source of your information?" You do this so often, time and again, that it becomes a natural habit of mind. Thus, debating is an excellent way to promote critical thinking. Without this capacity, we could be easily influenced, and in many instances, with undesirable outcomes, even negative personal consequences.

Thirdly, and most importantly, debating is about persuasion. People are persuaded for various reasons. For some, it is logic and rationality. For others, it is cultural, social, or even emotional. This awareness makes you more likely to be objective, rather than subjective, when making important decisions in your life.

Why is this a good idea?

For example, when a politician uses a slogan, such as, "Let's Change the World", you might ask, "What's Your Plan?" Rather than being swayed by the emotional prospect of a changed world, you now ask for substance. In essence, you are more objective, not easily persuaded by hollow phrases designed to appeal to you emotionally.

In conclusion, I have shared what I consider to be three important reasons why learning to debate is a good idea. In my book, "Teaching Debate in Chile, I list more reasons, and take a look at these reasons from various perspectives.

Finally, these three reasons, without the shadow of a doubt, are important for everyone. To put this as sincerely as possible, we all want to live in a better world. To do that, we need to know how to talk to one another when we are in disagreement. Therefore debate is a powerful tool to use. When we debate, peace, critical thinking and objectivity are all promoted. In today's world, and the better world of the future, these three aspects are, and will continue to be, highly desirable.

So practice...

Practice...

Practice...

That's what a debate coach does to develop great debaters!

http://bit.ly/JpzMRp

http://bit.ly/KAO7VI

http://bit.ly/KNmT3Z

## Chapter 15

## GENDER EQUALITY DEBATE

"In debate, **it is a great point to have the main point in mind**, and never to lose sight of it." ~ George Jacob Holyoake

*APEC recognizes that a successful society can result only from the full participation of women in the economy, and has strived to promote gender equality through such organizations as the Women Leaders Network (WLN) and the Gender Focal Point Network (GFPN). These and other bodies are charged with studying policy and promoting best practices regarding gender equality and making recommendations to APEC Ministers regarding how best to enable full participation of women in the economic and civic life of their societies.

As traditional economies and industries adopt more inclusive practices, it is important to reflect on the fundamental shifts necessary to achieve the successful implementation of gender equality.

In this regard, we must consider the cultural traditions, norms, and practices of the economies in which we conduct business, and the unique capabilities that women bring to the workplace.

Many women around the world are moving into senior management positions within large transnational corporations. For some APEC economies, this change in gender among the upper level staff might cause a bit of discomfort.

This teaching tip will allow students to debate gender issues arising in the current business environment.

**Content Objectives**

To debate gender discrimination in business

To apply the three rules of conduct for a debate

**Language Objectives**

To apply the language of agreement and disagreement in a respectful manner

To use the acronym A-R-E-T to plan, present, and justify one's position

**Activity**

1. Explain three rules for student behavior (Snider, 1999).

    a.  I will respect the rights of others to freedom of speech
    b.  I will respect my partners, opponents, and judges.
    c.  I will be a generous winner and a gracious loser.

2. Explain the acronym A-R-E-T to plan, present, and justify one's position (Baker, 2009):

**A**: Argument - A woman should receive the same salary as a man for the same job.

**R**: Reason(s) - A woman does the same quality and quantity of work as a man.

**E**: Evidence - A business manager, executive, or administrator does the same job, regardless of gender.

**T**: Therefore - Therefore, a woman ought to receive equal pay for equal work.

3. Explain the four speaking roles for each team:

1st Speaker (Captain) –

Outlines the main arguments the team will make.

2nd Speaker –
Presents the team's arguments for or against the topic.

3rd Speaker –
Presents the team's arguments for or against the topic.

4th Speaker –
Summarizes the team's arguments and closes the debate.

4. Explain the rules for turn-taking and timing:

a. The team in favor of the topic, pro, speaks first.
b. The team against the topic, con, speaks second.
c. Speakers alternate speaking turns until everyone has spoken.
d. All speakers speak for 3 minutes each.

5. The teacher describes and clarifies the chosen debate topic (see list of topics under Materials) and makes teams.

6. Ask which students would like to be pro (in agreement) and con (against).

7. Select four students to speak on each team.

8. Allow the students sufficient time to prepare their arguments together. (Students can use their notes but should not read their presentations word-for-word).

9. The two teams sit in front of the class to debate.

10. When they finish, the class members in the audience can question people on either team.

11. After the question and answer period, the audience votes on which team was the most convincing.

**Materials**

List of possible debate topics to choose from:

1. Women should receive the same salary as men for the same job.

2. Mothers who work outside the home neglect their children.

3. A woman should not receive a position that makes her the boss if the culture makes it difficult for a man to accept being subordinate to a woman.

4. If the number of female executives in a company is low, a woman should be promoted, even if the best applicant is a man.

5. Hiring a woman is a nightmare because of maternity leave and fears of sexual discrimination lawsuits. Equality laws, therefore, actually hold women in business back from economic opportunity.

**Category**
Women in Business: Gender discrimination

**Learning Theme**
Learning to do; problem solving

**\*What is APEC?**

According to Wikipedia, "Asia-Pacific Economic Cooperation (APEC) is a forum for 21 Pacific Rim countries (formally Member Economies) that seeks to promote free trade and economic cooperation throughout the Asia- Pacific region. Established in 1989 in response to the growing interdependence of Asia-Pacific economies and the advent of regional economic blocs (such as the European Union) in other parts of the world, APEC works to raise living standards and education levels through sustainable economic growth and to foster a sense of community and an appreciation of shared interests among Asia-Pacific countries. Members account for approximately 40% of the world's population, approximately 54% of the world's gross domestic product and about 44% of world trade. An annual APEC Economic Leaders' Meeting is attended by the heads of government of all APEC members except Taiwan (represented under the name Chinese Taipei) by aministerial-level official. The location of the meeting rotates annually among the member economies, and until 2011, a famous tradition involved the attending leaders dressing in a national costume of the host member.

## What kind of work does the Women Leaders Network (WLN) and the Gender Focal Point Network (GFPN) do?

These and other bodies are charged with studying policy and promoting best practices regarding gender equality and making recommendations to APEC Ministers regarding how best to enable full participation of women in the economic and civic life of their societies. As traditional economies and industries adopt more inclusive practices, it is important to reflect on the fundamental shifts necessary to achieve the successful implementation of gender equality. In this regard, we must consider the cultural traditions, norms, and practices of the economies in which we conduct business, and the unique capabilities that women bring to the workplace.

Many women around the world are moving into senior management positions within large transnational corporations. For some APEC economies, this change in gender among the upper level staff might cause a bit of discomfort. This teaching tip will allow students to debate gender issues arising in the current business environment.

## Resources
Baker, T. (2009). Debating in the EFL classroom. *International House Journal of Education and Development*, 27. Retrieved from ihjournal.com/debating-in-the-efl-classroom

Snider, A. (2008). *The code of the debater: Introduction to policy debating*. New York: International Debate Education Association.

Chapter 16

# DEBATERS, DEFINITIONS FIRST!

*"In debate, definitions are critical."*

# DEBATE, ARGUMENT, DIALOGUE, RHETORIC?

When two people, or two teams begin to debate something, an impartial observer often notices that the debate seems to be about two different things. The debaters energetically take their positions, delivering points and counterpoints. The clue to this divergence that we observe is that the teams have different understandings / interpretations of what they are debating.

Consequently, when the debate finishes, both teams legitimately feel like winners. After all, the other team failed to refute your argument. They never engaged with you because they had nothing to say, right?

Your rhetoric was robust, your arguments were awesome, your dialogue was delivered as both prologue and epilogue. You are clear that your team should definitely win the debate. You have left no doubt in anyone's mind... (Again, both teams feel this way)

To avoid this disappointment and the frustration it brings (for the teams, the adjudicators and the audience) debaters are required to not only define their terms, i.e. what the debate is about, but also to reach an agreement about what the key terms in the resolution (debate topic) mean when they use the key terms in the debate.

To not do this is called a, "**squirrel**", and it is frowned upon.

147

**Squirrels** basically want to "get the nut" for themselves, and a debater who "squirrels" or practices squirreling, is trying to make it impossible for the other team to have a fair chance to win.

Debates are supposed to be 50 – 50 propositions, not clear-cut, and therefore, the possibility of winning, or losing, is equal for both sides.

To win, you have to engage with the other side's arguments, clearly show those arguments are not true, not important, or will result in some undesirable negative consequences. On the other hand, your team's arguments are bigger, better, more important, and will result in some desirable consequence that outweighs any negatives that may be associated with it.

That's debating. That's what it's all about.

Argument,

Reason,

Evidence,

Consequences…

and Refutation of the other side's,

Argument,

Reason,

Evidence,

and consequences…

To do it right, to debate in this fashion, you have got to define your terms, or otherwise it gets to be quite ugly, with both sides having a one-way argument with…themselves.

Defining terms and reaching agreements about how those terms are being used is an imperative for a beautiful debate to take place…

http://bit.ly/KcAPTK

**

# THE FINAL DEBATE SPEECH: HOW TO DELIVER THE CLOSING ARGUMENT

The debate is almost over. You've got one more speech to make, the final one. What do you do?

What do you say? How do you say it? Does it even matter?

Let's face it, if you haven't been convincing by now, it's too late. Judges are humans. They make decisions based on first impressions, rarely on last impressions.

That's just the way humans are – we're "wired" that way. Where does it come from, this "make up your mind early" way of making decisions.

Answer: I don't know. But here's an experiment: Ask anybody, male or female – if they would consider dating someone who made a bad first impression. My guess is that 75% (for No) is a conservative estimate.

I have one more experiment for you. Ask anyone who has to interview people for a job, for employment. Ask that person if they would consider giving anyone a second interview – if they had a bad first impression. My guess is that 90% (again, No) is a conservative estimate.

What's my point? I'm simply trying to say if you have 2 speakers – a "weak" speaker and a "strong" speaker, then where you put the speakers matter.

If you're like most debate coaches, your weak speaker is first and your strong speaker is last.

Right?

It's human nature to "save the best for last". Well, in debating, don't do that. Do the opposite. Why?

Debating is a verbal sport, and as such, you want to "verbally hit" your opponent hard and often – before they hit you back.

Think of it like being in a physical battle.

Unless you are Muhammad Ali, do you really want to be "hit" by George Foreman, hard and often, until George gets tired, before you "hit" George?

Not me.

I put a sledgehammer in my gloves and go to pounding on George, hard and often, before he hits me. Many people speculate that Muhammad Ali suffered Parkinsons as a cumulative result of being hit, hard and often, by George Foreman and Joe Frazier.

What can we learn from this?

Don't let heavyweight punchers hit you – it's bad for your health. Seriously, I'm not kidding. Don't let other people "hit on you", neither in a boxing match, nor in a debating match. Defend yourself when you must, "hit your opponent" as hard as you can, whenever you can, as soon as you can, as often as you can. "Take the fight to the other team". Use your offense as your best defensive strategy.

Enough boxing metaphors. Let me be clear now.

In the evolution of the human race, species, early Cave Men had to make a split second "Friend or Foe", "Fight or Flight" decision every time they met a new person. This was our survival instinct. Well, we as a species, the human race has evolved, but the survival instinct is still intact.

We still have those survival tendencies. Quickly size up a person, decide whether or not someone is trustworthy, and quickly move on to other business.

Well, judges are humans. Don't make them wait until the end of a debate to find out you have a strong debater on your team. Let that strong debater speak first, and have the other debaters build on what was accomplished – through the use of the team line and the team split – and your final speaker – the "weak speaker" will have a wonderful time closing out the debate for your team.

On those rare occasions when the debate is evenly matched, a cohesive strategy – from beginning to end – keeping your arguments unified while constantly showing your arguments are bigger, more important, more relevant, cheaper, causing few drawbacks while achieving the greater good, the most benefits – then you will be in a positive position for the final speech, a winning speech.

Finally, what does a winning final speech look like, sound like, feel like? How do you stand and deliver this important speech?

Let me give you a scenario here:

You want to be the Prime Minister of Canada. OK? Prime Minister of Canada. Can you close your eyes and imagine that?

Great.

Next, the debate is now down to the final speech.

What would you say to the people of Canada?

Why should Canadians trust you? Is there anyone who they should distrust? What are you going to do that somebody else is not going to do?

Honestly, I don't have a clue. But take a moment to try to answer the questions. Then watch the video that follows. Listen to *what* they say. Listen to *how* they say *what* they say.

Next, turn the sound off. *Watch the body language.* Who is looking at you? Who is moving their hands in a natural manner? Who is reading a prepared speech to you?

Now, who do you trust? Who seems to have more **credibility**, more trustworthiness? Why?

Well, now you know. Now you know how to deliver a final speech, a closing argument. Now you can argue, without arguing...

Oh, I almost forgot. Here is the video. Just go to the website where the link takes you to. http://bit.ly/KcBncu

One more thing. Passively watching a video is a good way of learning, especially if you have chosen your video resource material wisely. Nonetheless, it goes without saying that simply watching someone else make an important speech is not going to be enough for you to be able to do the same.

You have got to put into practice the lessons you have learned through observation. Through diligent application of the principles and fundamentals of delivering an effective speech, you will increase your skill at this element of debating, namely, making the closing argument.

I have turned to the past to find a great speech, a conclusion to an important persuasive speech. The speech was made over 100 years ago by Daniel Webster, and has been all but forgotten. It suits our purposes well because it is the kind of speech that students can use to practice their ability to stand and deliver the closing argument.

It is the conclusion of Webster's speech, delivered in the United States Senate, on, *"The Presidential Veto of the United States Bank Bill"*. Notice the skillful interweaving of conviction and persuasion, and remember that this is the conclusion of a speech containing about 14,000 words. The speech to practice, reading aloud (not to be memorised), is as follows:

"Mr. President, we have arrived at a new epoch. We are entering on experiments, with the government and the Constitution of the country, hitherto untried, and of fearful and appalling aspect. This message calls us to the contemplation of a future which little resembles the past.

Its principles are at war with all that public opinion has sustained, and all which the experience of the government has sanctioned. It denies first principles; it contradicts truths, hitherto received as indisputable.

It denies to the judiciary the interpretation of law, and claims to divide with Congress the power of originating statutes. It extends the grasp of executive pretension over every power of the government. But this is not all.

It presents the chief magistrate of the Union in the attitude of arguing away the powers of that government over which he has been chosen to preside; and adopting for this purpose modes of reasoning which, even under the influence of all proper feeling towards high official station, it is difficult to regard as respectable.

It appeals to every prejudice which may betray men into a mistaken view of their own interests, and to every passion which may lead them to disobey the impulses of their understanding. It urges all the specious topics of State rights and national encroachment against that which a great majority of the States have affirmed to be rightful, and in which all of them have acquiesced.

It sows, in an unsparing manner, the seeds of jealousy and ill-will against that government of which its author is the official head. It raises a cry, that liberty is in danger, at the very moment when it puts forth claims to powers heretofore unknown and unheard of.

It affects alarm for the public freedom, when nothing endangers that freedom so much as its own unparalleled pretences. This, even, is not all.

It manifestly seeks to inflame the poor against the rich; it wantonly attacks whole classes of the people, for the purpose of turning against them the prejudices and the resentment of other classes.

It is a state paper which finds no topic too exciting for its use, no passion to inflammable for its address and its solicitation.

Such is this message. It remains now for the people of the United States to choose between the principles here avowed and their government.

These cannot subsist together. The one or the other must be rejected.

If the sentiments of the message shall receive general approbation, the Constitution will have perished even earlier than the moment which its enemies originally allowed for the termination of its existence. It will not have survived to its fiftieth year." [Source: Webster's Great Speeches, page 338.]

\*\*

There is little doubt that your students will have great fun delivering this speech. Not only that, because it contains masterful use of persuasive rhetoric to be used in the delivery of an effective conclusion. In other words, here is a speech worth studying to understand its powers of persuasion, on the one hand, and to interpret it through speech, on the other...

# Chapter 17

# THE RIGHT TO DIE:

*Are we - and should we be - in control of what happens at the end of our lives? Is there any such thing as the 'right' to die, and if so why should only the dying be granted it?*

## Debating in Chile's Public Schools

No, this is not an oxymoron. The terms, "debate" and "Chile" and "public school" are not mutually exclusive. There are some very good, sometimes even, great debates in Chile, in the public school sector. Firstly, here's a fundamental question:

### Why is debating a good idea?

There are a thousand answers to that question, and all of them are good. However, here's the answer that I like best:

"Why should we teach our students to debate, you ask? After all, debating is competitive, there's a winner and a loser. Shouldn't teachers be teaching their students how to cooperate, rather than compete?

Here's a global answer to the question(s):

"Sooner or later, all the people of the world will have to discover a way to live together in peace... If this is to be achieved, man must evolve for all human conflict a method which rejects

155

revenge, aggression, and retaliation..." ~ Dr. Martin Luther King, Jr. - 1964 Nobel Peace Prize Acceptance Speech

I'm sure you will agree that Dr. King's answer is both eloquent and powerful. So, we *are* convinced. Now, what about the debate in Chile?

This competition, organized by the English Opens Doors Program (Inglés Abre Puertas Program (PIAP), is aimed at students of Secondary Schools and the government funded municipal schools. The issue which was debated at this opportunity:

**"This House Believes That (THBT) the right to die is the ultimate personal freedom".**

Each team researches and prepares to debate, both in favor as well as against, before sorting the position they will have to defend. Here's the basic principle which serves as the foundation for this debate:

"All humans have rights, especially the right to dignity."

Universally, almost all people would quickly agree that human dignity is a basic human right that must be respected at all times.

But what happens when respecting someone's dignity – prevents you from saving someone's life?

That's what this debate is all about, namely: Do I have the right to take my own life, in a dignified manner, when I reach the conclusion that my life is no longer worth living because of some problem that is negatively affecting the quality of my life?

Do I have the right to die – as the ultimate expression of personal freedom???

A simple toss of the coin decides whether your team is pro (in favor) or contra (against).

**How will the debates turn out?**

I do not know. Winning a debate involves many aspects, so it's less important to focus on winning or losing. If you focus on how each member of the team makes an individual contribution to the success of the team, the results will always be favorable – win or lose.

**Why do I say that?**

Because debating is more about the skills you must develop in order to participate. A student must learn to research effectively, practice giving speeches, and be a good listener. These are skills that serve people throughout their entire lives, and that fact alone makes debating an outstanding activity, recommendable for all students.

More importantly, you learn to debate by debating. No matter what you do, debate. Research your topic, and then debate. If you are lucky, you will face a stronger opponent, and lose the debate. That is the moment when you will have to reflect about your performance, identify your strengths and weaknesses, and learn from your mistakes. Losing, in defeat, you will have your best teacher. Winning teaches the victors very little about debating.

Again, in debating, you enjoy the journey. It's not about winning, it's about participating. In the end, you will discover that everyone is a winner...

http://bit.ly/KcBncu

## Chapter 18

# DEATH PENALTY DEBATE

Debate Coach, you have just received the motion for your next debate. Your team needs to begin the process of preparing arguments for, and against, the motion. Here's the motion:

**"This House Believes That (THBT) the death penalty should be abolished."**

Well, the first thing you should do is hope that your team ends up debating the affirmative. This is a topic that lends itself well to the proposition team. Why? Quite frankly, no society on Earth condones the killing of human beings. We allow only three "exceptions": war, self-defense, and legal punishment. This third exception, legal punishment (a death sentence) is an exception that many feel should be eliminated.

Coach, if you are unlucky, your team must argue the negative. How can you possibly hope to win a debate in which you know the other team will be eloquent, well-researched, and genuinely PASSIONATE, emotionally involved, with their hearts, souls, and minds?

Let's be honest. You know you can't win, and your debaters know they can't win. So, you show up for the debate, make your speeches, and accept your loss. Right?

Wrong.

Firstly, debating isn't about winning or losing. If that's the approach you have been using, then it's time to stop. Now. Debating isn't, not now, nor has it ever been, a zero-sum game.

The motto, "if I win, you lose" is out of place in debating. Debating is about teaching young people to be critical thinkers, to see both sides of an issue, to express themselves clearly and articulately, and to make the world a better place for everyone to live in. Agreed?

So, let's go back to the Death Penalty debate. Review with your team the basics of debating: Ethos, Pathos, Logos. Your team will need to use all three in this debate, but especially "Logos" (logic).

The major strength of the affirmative team will be it's Pathos, (emotional appeal) to the judges and audience. As they point out the statistics, the case examples, and the inhumanity of one man killing another, everyone in the room will be mentally associating your team with the Death Penalty. So, what can you do?

**Answer: Turn the tables.**

Use "Ethos" (personal credibility) to rid yourself of the negative association being attributed to your team. Your team is only debating, they haven't put anyone to death, they haven't killed anyone, and have no plans to do so.

They go to church and believe in the Ten Commandments. Especially the one that says:

"Thou shalt not kill."

(Pause when you say that, while quickly scanning the room, looking everyone in the eye – a millisecond is enough)

In fact, we, and everyone in the room (said looking at the audience – using a broad, wide encircling, inclusive gesture that terminates with the speaker touching their heart – earnest look on face) we all, everyone in this room, we all believe killing is not right.

"Let's be clear, this is only a debate"…

(End of speech)

Coach, your team is now able to go forward with your "Logos", your logic. You begin to go to your statistics, your facts, your figures, all the while making it clear that you live in a society in which everyone believes that no man should kill another man. (You already got the judges, the audience, and even the other team to accept this).

Well, it is not enough to believe this. You must make the choice about how this belief is best protected, and best achieved. That entails making a difficult decision.

That is where we "clash" today. The proposition believes that *even if* one man kills another man, a killer has the right to expect that no man will kill the killer.

The proposition is asking the judges, the audience, to accept that the killer has a right to the protection of a society that believes no man should kill another man.

We clash today because we believe that a killer did not believe in, and did not practice the right to life. The action of the killer clearly shows they do not believe what you and I believe. You and I believe that the right to life is sacred. We believe the right to life is universal. A murderer does not believe in these things.

Therefore, the opposition believes that a killer has forfeited the right to life, and that the biblical doctrine of, "an eye for an eye" should be applied. In fact, to be consistent with our civilized society, based on the fundamental belief in the right to life, the death penalty must be applicable. (*This is your argument*)

In other words, the death penalty is justified as the only penalty possible for anyone who kills another human being. A society who believes life is precious, a society who believes life is sacred, a society who believes no man should kill another man, then *such* a society must accept the unavoidable ultimate consequence of its belief, the death penalty for murderers. Thank you. (*end of speech*)

Debate Coach, now your team has made the debate an even debate. The proposition has *Pathos*, or emotion, on their side. Your team has used *Ethos* (we are not killers) and *Logos* (Logic: society is responsible to hold all life **sacred**, not permit killers to **desecrate** the **sanctity of human life** without paying an equal price-their own life) to counteract their advantage.

From here on out, this would be a great debate. Remember, it's not a zero-sum game. It's not about winning, it's about developing the ability to critically examine an issue, and then reach your own conclusions.

Finally, I've got a great link with some great information about the death penalty. Yes, you must do your research, so the link is **only a starting point.**

Don't forget human, eye to eye, face to face research. Get your team out there talking to victims of crimes, talking to their neighbors, talking to lawyers, judges, doctors, priests and pastors.

Debating, in the end, always comes down to how real people are affected by the issues of the day. You have got to go talk to them, if you wish to speak for them. Oh, here's the link:

Death penalty statistics from the US: which state executes the most people? http://bit.ly/rixBjm

Barack Obama on the Death Penalty: http://bit.ly/Jpxm5k

Question:

If your wife, your husband, or your child child was raped and murdered, would you be in favor of the death penalty?

Click this link for the surprising answer... http://bit.ly/Ksah0v

\*\*

# Chapter 19

# CAPITAL PUNISHMENT: PRO OR CONTRA

*"We are what we repeatedly do. Excellence then, is not an act, but a habit." ~ Aristotle*

In my first debate book, "Teaching Debate in Chile" I covered the basics of debate. With it, a debate coach could more than adequately prepare their team for a debate. What is missing from the book however, is advanced coverage of common debate topics. The purpose of this chapter, and indeed this book, is to address the common debate topics that are often used. In this way, a debate team can reduce significantly the amount of time needed to prepare for a debate.

What that means is that more time can be spent preparing the team for the delivery of the speeches. As you will remember from the previous book, debates are judged on three things:

- **content,**

- **style,** and

- **strategy**.

Using this book wisely will give you more time to work on **style** (speech delivery), while allowing you to quickly decide on matters of **content** and **strategy**.

How does this work? First, there is a poll / survey for you to do. This is your data collection. It provides the debaters with statistics, facts and figures taken randomly, from everyday people who you meet on the street.
**On the street?**

Yes, on the street. You are talking to real people, face to face. It is important to find out information from real people about how they feel, what their their opinions are, how they are affected, and their genuine reactions to the issues of the day. So, yes, get out on the street and talk to people. Real people. For example:

**You**: Hi. I'm doing a survey / taking a poll about _____ . Would you mind taking a minute to answer some questions for me?"

**Real Person**: No problem...

\*\*

Again, as I mentioned above, go on the street, ask for help, and you will be surprised how many people really stop to help you. Remember, this empirical evidence can be used effectively in the preparation and delivery of your debate speeches.

Second, there are four short videos which will examine both sides of the debate topic. This may be done in any manner that presents the issue so that the fundamental principles at stake are clear and understandable.

Thus, insights into how a team might approach the delivery of an effective speech can be gained through careful observation.

That's all there is to it. Ready to give it a go? Let's begin. Good luck in your debate!

**"Justice is blind"**

# DEBATE 1:

# MOTION:

# THIS HOUSE BELIEVES THAT THE DEATH PENALTY SHOULD NOT BE USED UNDER ANY CIRCUMSTANCES

Let's go to our poll / survey for research data. What do the people say?

How many people agree? What percent?

How many people disagree? What percent?

What percent give an alternate answer?

Are there any interesting comments?

Examine the survey data looking for trends that might support your position.

Next, it's time for both teams to go through six (6) **fundamental steps** to *build their case.*

"What makes a decent World School Debating Championships (WSDC) case?" (Excerpt)

19 November 2008
Poslal Andrej Schulcz
http://bit.ly/p8uplq

**An article on what to think of during case building.**

The World Schools Debating Championship uses a format that has become as open as never before. There is no single debate strategy that beats all different ones. Nonetheless, the format has also developed a tradition, which now most judges at Worlds expect the teams to follow. This tradition is not unjustified.

On the contrary, it is a tradition of best practice what to look for in case construction before a debate and presenting the case in the twelve or so minutes in the first and second speeches.

This article will attempt to sum up what is expected of debate cases at Worlds, so that debaters will no longer be surprised by the elegance of how other teams state their arguments. In short, what makes a decent WSDC case?

MOTION:

**The death penalty should not be used under any circumstances.**

Yes or No

Do you agree? Do you disagree?

Consider this possible exception to include in your case:

"Death penalty possible if victim's family asks for capital punishment. Since they have suffered the loss of a family member, directly, the family should have the option to demand capital punishment."

<u>Yes or No</u>

Do you agree? Do you disagree?

Basically, this is a **checklist** of what you should look for in preparation, and what should be included in the first speech of your team, especially if you are in the **proposition**.

While the international rules require only some of the listed items to be included, and they state no order in which they should be presented, all of them should be dealt with in one way or the other, and for less experienced debaters it is better to mention them explicitly, **rather than leave too much to the judge's imagination**.

## 1. Introducing the debate

Funny or serious, examples or generalizations, this is a moment for style. No natter what your style is, make it clear to the judges why the debate topic is important. Be clear about why it matters, and to whom.

## 2. Defining what the debate should be about

Define the key terms of the debate. Be explicit. Use an authoritative dictionary, current year edition. Alternatively, set the parameters, or borders, of the debate. This lets the judges and the opposing team know what you define as being outside the limits of the debate topic.

## 3. Specifying the team's position

Now it's time to clearly state your position you will stand for, or against. This plan is called a "**model**" and can accept all, or parts of the debate motion. In our death penalty debate, for example, you can accept that it is 100% eliminated, no death penalty in no circumstance, or you could name exceptions in which you would apply the death penalty (war crimes, mass murderers, child murderers, when police are killed, etc.)

The opposing side can also do the same, in effect making a counter-proposal, instead of simply opposing the death penalty. In such a case, the opposing team is conceding the point, (no death penalty) but attempting to prove they have a better plan, or model, that is bigger, better, cheaper, or more beneficial than what the other team is proposing to do.

Note, this is the format of the World Schools Debating Championships (WSDC), an international competition. You will have to check your local rules to see if any restrictions apply on your local, regional, or national level. In sum, the judges, and the opposing team expect to be clearly told what your plan (model) is. This is absolutely necessary.

## 4. **Presenting the team line**

This is a sentence, or line, that everyone on the team will say.

This is the 'big picture' to your case." Work on your individual arguments first, and the big idea, will emerge naturally. This team line unites all the speeches, and is strategically important.

For instance, in the motion, "This House Believes That the death penalty should not be used under any circumstances", the proposition could say: "We will uphold the right to life and avoid irrevocable errors, – You can't say, "Sorry" to a dead man who was innocent!

The opposition would state their team line explicitly, saying perhaps, "The decision is difficult, but the death penalty is the only adequate solution for a society that values the lives of its members!

## 5. Splitting the case

This is simply, *who* speaks, on *what* topics.

To illustrate, in this death penalty debate, the first speaker of the proposition may not want to simply say that their team will have an **economic** and a **moral argument**, and one about the **quality** of life improsonment, but be a bit more creative.

Instead, they could say: "I will look at why our model is needed for **financial reasons**, and why this is the **just model**, and **our second speaker** will talk about **how it will improve the quality** of justice for society in general and the murderer in particular."

## 6. Presenting the arguments

Finally, you focus on the *persuasive force* of the arguments.

You can do this since you have quickly put your case together, by stating your **definitions,** your **model** and your **case division** (team split) properly. Again, the aim of this Advanced Debating chapter is not to make your arguments for you, but to make your case preparation efficient.

You know what must be done, what is needed, and you do it, leaving your team with ample time to master your arguments. Once you get used to this process of rapid debate preparation, you don't have to focus on what makes a good case, but what makes a good debate – the arguments...

\*\*

Jeremy Irons talks about the death penalty: http://bit.ly/LscXvg

California's Death Penalty: "The death penalty is not about justice, it's about revenge." http://bit.ly/KcHRIg

\*\*

CAPITAL PUNISHMENT (CP) (Practice Debate)

Motion: Capital Punishment should be abolished in the USA.

INTRODUCTION

I. There is at the present time considerable sentiment in the United States in favor of the total abolition of capital punishment.

II. The number of offences punishable by death is continually decreasing.

III. Certain foreign countries, and some of the territories of the United States, have already passed laws prohibiting CP.

IV. The question at issue is: Should this prohibition be extended to every state in the USA?

AFFIRMATIVE TEAM (Abolish Capital Punishment)

I. Capital punishment is unnecessary; for,—

A. Justice may be secured by imprisonment; for,—
1. Society is adequately protected by the incarceration of the offender.

B. Life imprisonment is more feared by criminals than death itself; for,—
1. It often inflicts greater suffering upon the victim.

II. Capital punishment has evil effects upon the community; for,—
A. It diminishes the sacredness in which human life is, held, for,—
1. If the State claims that it is justified in killing those of its citizens who commit given offences, then individuals feel that they are justified for taking life under similar circumstances.

B. It tends to lower the moral sense of the public; for,—

1. Capital punishment is usually accompanied by lots of publicity.
2. Capital punishment methods are cruel (e.g., electrocution).

C. It causes such public sympathy that justice is thwarted; for,—
1. Juries often acquit a man rather than sentence him to death.

III. Capital punishment is unsound sociologically; for,—

A. It does not try to reform the prisoner; for,—
1. Death usually follows closely upon conviction.

B. It arouses the worst passions in men; for,—
1. It is barbaric: "an eye for an eye, and a tooth for a tooth."

IV. Capital punishment is not practical; for,—
A. It has completely failed to stop crime ; for,—
1. Statistics show that where capital punishment is *in force*, crime is on the increase.

V. Reform methods should replace capital punishment; for,—

A. Such methods are sound sociologically.

B. Such methods are more humane.

C. Such methods actually decrease crime.

\*\*\*

NEGATIVE TEAM (Keep Capital Punishment)

I. Capital punishment is desirable for society; for,—
A. It insures a speedy and effective remedy in those cases where grave crimes are committed against the State.

B. It is the only real preventive of crime; for,—

1. Statistics show that where capital punishment *has been abolished*, crime has greatly increased.

C. It is more economical; for,—

1. It saves the expense of guarding and housing many prisoners.

D. It prevents hardened criminals from being again permitted to commit more crimes.

II. Capital punishment is desirable for criminals themselves; for,—

A. Its severity acts as a deterrent of crime; for,—

1. If a person knows he will be killed if he commits a murder, he is more likely to keep his passions under control than he would be if he would be only imprisoned, with the possibility of pardon later on.

B. It is more humane than life imprisonment; for,—

1. It disposes of the criminal simply and quickly.

III. The objections against capital punishment are not valid; for,—

A. The lives of innocent persons are rarely taken; for,—

1. Courts do not inflict death penalty unless the evidence is conclusive. The death sentence is always reviewed by higher courts.

B. Capital punishment is used only for the most severe crimes; for,—

1. Imprisonment is sufficient for minor crimes.

C. The State must be severe to maintain law and order; for,—

1. A laxity of law enforcement or lenient regulations would result in a great increase in crime; perhaps in anarchy.

2. The State must protect its citizens, no matter how severe a penalty is necessary.

# Chapter 20

## THIS HOUSE BELIEVES SMOKING SHOULD BE PROHIBITED IN ALL PUBLIC PLACES

Time to debate again. You've got a topic:

**This house that smoking should be prohibited in all public places.**

There are two teams. One is the **affirmative** team. That means you are for the topic. This team must present clear and compelling arguments why smoking should be prohibited in all public places.

The other team is the **negative** team. This team is against the topic. They must present clear and compelling arguments why smoking should NOT be prohibited in all public places.

That isn't all, however. If both teams only present arguments to prove their point of view, then what you have isn't a debate.

It's more like two car salesmen trying to sell you a car. You are going to buy a car. Now, which car is the best car, when both are good?

Well, the salesman who is more persuasive will sell the car to you.

So, what makes this a debate? The same thing that a car salesperson would do if they learned you were considering buying another car. What would they do?

First, they would tell you why the other car, the one you are considering buying, is a bad car. They would convince you the other car is totally wrong for you. They would leave no doubt in your mind that the other car is a bad decision.

Then they would tell you why the car they have is the best car. You'd hear about best price, comfort, speed, status, durability and of course, low gas mileage. Then you would hear about tax benefits. Of course you can have the car in any color you want.

Air conditioning is possible too for the hot summer months. You can also expect low maintenance costs, nothing to worry about. Testimonials from other satisfied car owners would be made available if you want someone to talk to.

To finish, there comes the test drive.

You were born to be wild. Put your shades on. Get your motor running, head out on the highway, wind in your face, your hair flying freely like a rock star, turn up the music, born to be wild, yeaah baby!

Pulling back in the car lot after an exhilarating test drive, you are sold. Time to sign the papers. You just bought yourself a car.

Sorry, I meant a debate. You just won the debate. You have got to destroy the other teams' reasons, and put your own reasons in the best possible light. You do that with clear, convincing, and compelling arguments.

You are like a lawyer, for example, defending a client in a murder trial. Your client is innocent. How is it possible for your client to be in two places at the same time? Innocent is the only verdict possible. No matter what the other lawyer says, to commit the crime, you have to be at the crime scene. Innocent.

Ladies and gentlemen, that is clear and compelling evidence. That's what you do in a debate. You bring the strongest arguments you have. Leave the weak arguments on Google. (really) Oh, and don't forget. Destroy the other team's argument.

Now, you can play it safe and attack all the arguments. But identify the main argument, attack it successfully, and all the other arguments are irrelevant. They don't matter because you proved that your client wasn't at the crime scene.

The gloves, the murder weapon, even the DNA don't matter. How can DNA not matter? How can a murder weapon not matter? How can a bloody pair of shoes not matter?

That's easy. Someone else put them there.

It wasn't your client. Your client wasn't there.

No person can be in two places at the same time.

So what's the verdict? Only one is possible: Innocent.

So dear debaters, never fail to recognize what is the most important thing you have to prove, and then prove it. Otherwise, you will end up with empty hands.

Good luck in your debate, to both teams. By the way, you do know that you have to prepare for both sides of the debate, right? How do you expect to win, if you don't know what the other team is going to say, before they say it?

Prepare for both sides of the debate. It's crucial. Besides, you don't know if you are the affirmative team, or if you will be the negative team. A flip of the coin decides that.

Now, before I close, here are some links to some great resource material:

http://bit.ly/JUa88t   http://bit.ly/qWSjHy

# Chapter 21

# MALCOLM X DEBATES AT OXFORD

# "EXTREMISM IN THE DEFENSE OF LIBERTY IS NO VICE"

Malcolm X participated in a classic debate at Oxford Union, a special all university organization as part of Oxford University in England. The debate took place December 3, 1964.

He speaks in favor of the motion that, "extremism in the defense of liberty is no vice".

Do you coach a debate team? Do you use debate with your students, from time to time? Then your students surely have to watch debates on video, right? I know my students watch an incredible number of debates, and a wide variety of speakers and speeches. Why?

Answer:   Style. Rhetoric. Delivery. Rhythm. Ethos, Pathos, Logos.

Few speakers in few speeches, few debaters in few debates do what the following speaker did, namely, everything.

If you try to explain it, you will surely attribute it to the urgency of the moment. Immediacy is often the inspiration for extraordinary speeches. This is true for this speech. The speaker was living in a historically urgent time, the African-American struggle for Civil Rights in the USA.

The times were revolutionary ones, transformational ones. The struggle for Civil Rights would leave nobody in the USA indifferent, without an opinion or uncaring of the outcome. It was the time of the great struggle for Civil Rights in the USA, promised a 100 years earlier, in the Emancipation Proclamation, but never a true reality.

Indeed, many would point out that at the time, the state of civil rights in the USA was a direct contradiction of the principle of the right to life, liberty, and the pursuit of happiness enshrined by its Founding Fathers. As Dr. Martin Luther would eloquently put it, I paraphrase: America has issued the Negro a bad check. It has come back from the bank marked, "insufficient funds." America has defaulted on its promise." (see King's, "I Have A Dream" speech).

That is the context of the speech in this debate, the Civil Rights Struggle, definitely an urgent time for any African-American. But it doesn't explain the greatness of Malcolm's speech. Some other quality must be invoked.

I call it **passion**, mixed with **intellect**, mixed with **audacity**, mixed with **eloquence**.

Rhetoric, delivery, presence, rhythm, cadence, logic, intellect, this can be called many things. I would most likely agree with your assessment.

Beyond that, in any case, this is a video that a debater is required to study, for it holds many secrets of persuasive speech...

Enjoy Malcolm X, debating at Oxford University in 1964.

You'll hear X's trademark claim that liberty can be attained by **"whatever means necessary,"** including force, if the government won't guarantee it, and that "intelligently directed extremism" will achieve liberty far more effectively than pacifist strategies. (He's clearly alluding to Martin Luther King.)

I'd also encourage you to watch the dramatic closing minutes and pay some attention to the nice rhetorical slide, where X takes lines from Shakespeare's "Hamlet" and uses them to justify his own position when he uses the phrase, "by whatever means necessary".

You'd probably never expect to see Hamlet getting invoked that way, let alone Malcolm X speaking at Oxford. This is in and of itself a wonderful set of contrasts to be aware of. Let's go to the speech now:

**Malcolm X**: "I read once, passingly, about a man named Shakespeare. I only read about him passingly, but I remember one thing he wrote that kind of moved me. He put it in the mouth of Hamlet, I think, it was, who said, 'To be or not to be.'

He was in doubt about something—whether it was nobler in the mind of man to suffer the slings and arrows of outrageous fortune—moderation—or to take up arms against a sea of troubles and by opposing end them.

And I go for that. If you take up arms, you'll end it, but if you sit around and wait for the one who's in power to make up his mind that he should end it, you'll be waiting a long time.

And in my opinion, the young generation of whites, blacks, browns, whatever else there is, you're living at a time of extremism, a time of revolution, a time when there's got to be a change.

People in power have misused it, and now there has to be a change and a better world has to be built, and the only way it's going to be built—is with extreme methods.

And I, for one, will join in with anyone—I don't care what color you are—as long as you want to change this miserable condition that exists on this earth." December 3, 1964

Watch the video: http://bit.ly/P6bvx

**

Chapter 22

WHAT EVERY DEBATE COACH SHOULD
KNOW

(Quote) *"Argumentation is the art of presenting truth so that others will accept it and act in accordance with it."*

~ Goerge K. Pattee, A. M., Assistant Professor of English and Rhetoric, Pennsylvania State College, and author of, *"Practical Argumentation"*, (1909)

Over a hundred years ago, George K. Pattee wrote a book about argumentation that is as good as any other book about debating that you can find today, including the one you are reading now. In his book, Professor Pattee identified and addressed some key elements for debaters.

His table of contents includes the following topics: persuasion, conviction, and speech preparation, among others. This is essential information for any debate coach, in any time period, past, present or future, to know. Accordingly, this book has taken care to adequately address these issues from various perspectives.

It would be well worth our time to allow Professor Pattee to "speak" in his own voice, so that we may take full advantage of a teacher who was interested in the practical side of argumentation, and not merely a theorist. As I have shown throughout this book, it is in the actual practice of debating in which one becomes skilled at debating. So, we are well advised to take a closer look at what he has to say:

Professor George K. Pattee, A. M. (Quoted excerpt, pp. 5-9, 1909) "The practical benefit to be derived from the study and application of the principles of argumentation can hardly be overestimated. The man who wishes to influence the opinions and actions of others, who wishes to become a leader of men in however great or however humble a sphere, must be familiar with this art.

The editor, the lawyer, the merchant, the contractor, the laborer--men in every walk of life--depend for their success upon bringing others to believe, in certain instances, as they believe. Everywhere men who can point out what is right and best, and can bring others to see it and act upon it, win the day.

Another benefit to be obtained from the study of argumentation is the ability to be convinced intelligently. The good arguer is not likely to be carried away by specious arguments or fallacious reasoning. He can weigh every bit of evidence; he can test the strength and weakness of every statement; he can separate the essential from the unessential; and he can distinguish between prejudice and reason. A master of the art of argumentation can both present his case convincingly to others, and discover the truth in a matter that is presented to him.

Argumentation can hardly be considered as a distinct art standing by itself; it is rather a composite of several arts, deriving its fundamentals from them, and depending upon them for its existence. In the first place, since argumentation is spoken or written discourse, it belongs to rhetoric, and the rules which govern composition apply to it as strongly as to any other kind of expression.

In fact, perhaps rhetorical principles should be observed in argumentation more rigidly than elsewhere, for in the case of narration, description, or exposition, the reader or hearer, in an endeavor to derive pleasure or profit, is seeking the author, while in argumentation it is the author who is trying to force his ideas upon the audience. Hence an argument must contain nothing crude or repulsive, but must be attractive in every detail.

In the second place, any composition that attempts to alter beliefs must deal with reasons, and the science of reasoning is logic. There is no need for the student of argumentation to make an exhaustive study of this science, for the good arguer is not obliged to know all the different ways the mind may work; he must, however, know how it should work in order to produce trustworthy results, and to the extent of teaching correct reasoning, argumentation includes logic.

In the third place, a study of the emotions belongs to argumentation. According to the definition, argumentation aims both at presenting truth and compelling action. As action depends to a great extent upon man's emotions, the way to arouse his feelings and passions is a fundamental principle of this art. Argumentation, then, which is commonly classified as the fourth division of rhetoric, consists of two fundamental elements.

The part that is based upon logic and depends for its effectiveness upon pure reasoning is called – conviction -; the part that consists of an emotional appeal to the people addressed is called – persuasion - .

If the only purpose of argumentation were to demonstrate the truth or falsity of a hypothesis, conviction alone would be sufficient. But its purpose is greater than this: it aims both (1) to convince men that certain ideas are true, and also (2) to persuade them to act in accordance with the truth presented. Neither conviction nor persuasion can with safety be omitted.

An appeal to the intellect alone may demonstrate principles that cannot be refuted; it may prove beyond a doubt that certain theories are logical and right, and ought to be accepted. But this sort of argument is likely to leave the person addressed cold and unmoved and unwilling to give up his former ideas and practices.

A purely intellectual discourse upon the evils resulting from a high tariff would scarcely cause a life-long protectionist to change his politics. If, however, some emotion such as duty, public spirit, or patriotism were aroused, the desired action might result.

Again it frequently happens that before the arguer can make any appeal to the logical faculties of those he wishes to influence, he will first have to use persuasion in order to gain their attention and to arouse their interest either in himself or in his subject.

On the other hand, persuasion alone is undoubtedly of even less value than conviction alone.

A purely persuasive argument can never be trusted to produce lasting effects. As soon as the emotions have cooled, if no reasonable conviction remains to guide future thought and action, the plea that at first seemed so powerful is likely to be forgotten.

The preacher whose sermons are all persuasion may, for a time, have many converts, but it will take something besides emotional ecstasy to keep them "in good and regular standing."

The proportion of conviction and persuasion to be used in any argumentative effort depends entirely upon the attending circumstances. If the readers or hearers possess a high degree of intelligence and education, conviction should predominate; for it is a generally accepted fact that the higher man rises in the scale of civilization, the less he is moved by emotion.

A lawyer's argument before a judge contains little except reasoning; before a jury persuasion plays an important part.

In the next place, the arguer must consider the attitude of those whom he would move. If they are favorably disposed, he may devote most of his time to reasoning; if they are hostile, he must use more persuasion. Also the correct proportion varies to some extent according to the amount of action desired.

In an intercollegiate debate where little or no action is expected to result, persuasion may almost be neglected; but the political speech or editorial that urges men to follow its instructions usually contains at least as much persuasion as conviction.

The aspirant for distinction in argumentation should study and acquire certain characteristics common to all good arguers. First of all, he should strive to gain the ability to analyze.

No satisfactory discussion can ever take place until the contestants have picked the question to pieces and discovered just exactly what it means. The man who does not analyze his subject is likely to seize upon ideas that are merely connected with it, and fail to find just what is involved by the question as a whole. The man skillful in argumentation, however, considers each word of the proposition in the light of its definition, and only after much thought and study decides that he has found the real meaning of the question.

But the work of analysis does not end here; every bit of proof connected with the case must be analyzed that its value and its relation to the matter in hand may be determined. Many an argument is filled with what its author thought was proof, but what, upon close inspection, turns out to be mere assertion or fallacious reasoning.

This error is surpassed only by the fault of bringing in as proof that which has no direct bearing at all upon the question at issue.

Furthermore, the arguer must analyze not only his own side of the discussion but also the work of his opponent, so that with a full knowledge of what is strong and what is weak he may make his attack to the best advantage.

Next to the ability to analyze, the most important qualification for an arguer to possess is the faculty of clearly presenting his case.

New ideas, new truths are seldom readily accepted, and it is never safe to assume that the hearer or the reader of an argument will laboriously work his way through a mass of obscure reasoning.

Absolute clearness of expression is essential. The method of arriving at a conclusion should be so plain that no one can avoid seeing what is proved and how it is proved. Lincoln's great success as a debater was due largely to his clearness of presentation.

In the third place, the person who would control his fellow men must assume qualities of leadership. Remembering that men can be led, but seldom be driven, he must show his audience how he himself has reached certain conclusions, and then by leading them along the same paths of reasoning, bring them to the desired destination.

If exhortation, counsel, and encouragement are required, they must be at his command. Moreover, a leader who wishes to attract followers must be earnest and enthusiastic. The least touch of insincerity or indifference will ruin all.

To analyze ideas, to present them clearly, and as a leader to enforce them enthusiastically and sincerely are necessary qualities for every arguer.

A debater should possess additional attainments. He ought to be a ready thinker. The disputant who depends entirely upon a set speech is greatly handicapped. Since it is impossible to tell beforehand just what arguments an opponent will use and what line of attack he will pursue, the man who cannot mass his forces to meet the requirements of the minute is at great disadvantage.

Of course all facts and ideas must be mastered beforehand, but unless one is to be the first speaker, he can most effectually determine during the progress of the debate just what arguments are preferable and what their arrangement should be.

A debater must also have some ability as a speaker. He need not be graceful or especially fluent, though these accomplishments are of service, but he must be forceful. Not only his words, but also his manner must reveal the earnestness and enthusiasm he feels.

His argument, clear, irrefutable, and to the point, should go forth in simple, burning words that enter into the hearts and understanding of his hearers." (end of quoted excerpt)

\*\*

As we have seen, debating is a worthwhile activity for students to learn. It does not matter what occupation a student may eventually choose as a career path. We can say with absolute and total certainty that debating will be useful throughout the entire course of someone's lifetime.

I have presented this information as a *voice from the past*. I strongly believe that every debate coach should be clear about debating as an enriching experience for participants. If this is the case, the debate coach will be a source of enthusiasm and motivation for students to emulate.

As is often the case, and rightfully so, students' attitudes towards, and enjoyment of, any activity is directly influenced by the leadership of the teacher. In this case, the debate coach is responsible for providing the kind of leadership that clearly demonstrates to students that learning to debate is a great investment in their future that will provide many positive returns.

This book has shown examples from contemporary times, and times gone by, of how knowledge gained in debating can be applied practically to the lives of ourselves (debate coach) and our students. Long after the last debate is finished, the positive effects of debating will linger on in our lives.

If we truly desire to make a better world, debating provides us with a possibility to equip our students with the necessary capacity to enter into constructive dialogue with people whom we may disagree with. The more we are able to do this, the more likely we will move towards a world that can live in peace with those whom we have differences of opinion.

Finally, no matter how or why you became a debate coach, you can make a difference. After the initial shock wears off from suddenly becoming the new Debate Society coach, you can begin to use this book to help you recruit, train and establish a positive debating program at your school. Above all, if nothing else, recognise the transformative potential of debate, and provide a positive learning experience for your students. Everything else will ultimately take care of itself...

**

# Appendix:

# The Question of the Minimum Wage in 1913

### Resolved:

**That through appropriate legislation, a minimum wage scale ought to be put into operation in the United States.**

### THE CONSTRUCTIVE AND REBUTTAL SPEECHES OF BAKER UNIVERSITY

## A. R. Bradley, First Affirmative Speaker (Baker University)

Honorable Judges, Ladies and Gentlemen: Nations perish when their foundations crumble. Hence a question of vital concern to our laboring class must necessarily vitally concern our nation; for the great laboring class constitutes the basis of society. The wide spread interest which this question is arousing and the action which has been started in several states forces it upon the minds of the thinking public with a burning appeal. Following the example of Massachusetts nine states have enrolled on their statute books a minimum wage law. Hence, we are face to face with living progressive truths, no longer theories.

Industrial disputes are about the only form of contention in which the government does not arbitrarily compel adjustment, but even these are coming more and more under the jurisdiction of the state until at present two-thirds of our states have some form of law concerning labor and its interests. Why this increasing interest? There is a vast horde of laborers in the United States who are forced by starvation wages to exist among such sordid surroundings that they are wrecked in character and in physique, the greatest assets of a nation. In spite of the fact that through the long weary hours of toil they have produced wealth and luxury for their employers, these miserable beings are doomed to suffer for the lack of the things they themselves have created.

Slavery has not been abolished, friends, until all such disgraces as exist in our industrial world have been eradicated. All enlightened society from Massachusetts to Oregon is demanding that a remedy be found for the evil of the low wage. The fundamental principle of labor legislation is the conservation of the human resources of our nation, hence the wage question, because of what it involves, becomes one of our greatest national problems.

Ladies and gentlemen, in our presentation of the minimum wage we do not contend for some visionary adjustment which will force industry out of business and establish labor in luxury. We contend that upon no other basis than that of complete justice to both

186

employer and employee can this question ever be settled, and it is upon such a basis that we present the minimum wage. We shall not argue that a minimum wage shall be arbitrarily fixed as a living wage, but we base our contention for a minimum as such a wage that will be just and fair to both employer and worker.

We concede that starvation wages are not the sole causes of poverty and wretchedness of the laborer, but statistics and investigation prove beyond contention that a vast army of workers, especially the unskilled, are forced to toil for existence under conditions destructive to physical and moral being. The negative must concede this fact, and that a society based on such labor, whatever temporary success it may attain, must come to final degradation and ruin.

Likewise, Honorable Judges, the proposition as stated does not necessarily mean that a minimum wage apply to each and all industries. We admit that the highly skilled and well organized trades may not need it, and therefore we shall contend at no time that wages as a whole shall be tampered with or regulated. However, we do contend that a vast number of workers must be protected by this means against their own ignorance and helplessness as well as against the greed of the employers.

In this class are found the sweated laborer, the underpaid factory worker, women and children, and such industries as are dependent upon the mercy of employers. We do not advocate that a laborer should be paid more than he earns. That would be injustice to the employer. Our sole contention is that if labor is exploited and underpaid, as we shall prove, then in the name of eternal justice some remedy must be found and applied.

We realize that the plan, being a human device, is not perfect, therefore our argument is for the principle involved and can not be disproved by an attack on the minor details.

Now, Honorable Judges, having given you our conception and understanding of minimum wage I will now prove to you that the minimum wage becomes a necessity. That capital is to a deplorable extent oppressing labor in our country is an admitted fact.

According to Professor Nearing, one of the world's greatest authorities on wage problems, one per cent of our population controls fifty per cent of the wealth of our country and further more than fifty-one per cent of the laborers of our country have an annual income of less than $625, a sum estimated by some of our authorities as being barely sufficient to maintain American standards.

With these facts in mind we see that labor is receiving a pitifully small proportion of that which it produces.

It is impossible to believe that one per cent has produced as much as the other ninety-nine per cent. The report of the Bureau of Industrial Statistics of Pennsylvania shows that in seven trades employing more than 60,000 women the average yearly wage is less than $300.

Since a large per cent earn more than the average it follows, of necessity, that a great number earn less than this pitiful sum. According to a report of a government investigation in the state of Connecticut in the cotton industry 29 per cent earn less than $7, the base fixed by this commission as a living wage; 58 per cent earn less than that in the silk, 49 per cent in the metal and 49.5 per cent in the rubber, or 48.4 per cent of the combined labor in these industries fall below the standard of $7. It is evident, therefore, that nearly one-half receive less than a living wage.

Honorable Judges, these figures were copied from the pay rolls and embodied in this report to the government. The question arises, can the industries afford to pay more? A comparison of wages and the value of the products shows that labor receives less than 22 per cent of the value of the product which it creates.

Who would contend that this is a fair proportion?

A startling fact is shown by Adams and Sumner in their book, "Wage Problems," that wages in the sweated industries have decreased in the last decade. This statement has actually been verified by investigations. Since this is true it is clearly seen that conditions demand legislative adjustment.

Again, quoting Professor Nearing, whose research is extensive and whose findings are without bias, one-fourth of the men and four-fifths of the women of the state of New Jersey receive less than $468 per year.

Ladies and gentlemen, I might present a labyrinth of figures proving that labor in this country is underpaid, but these facts, taken from governmental investigations in several representative states, proves beyond the shadow of a doubt that more action, for the protection of American standards of living is essential. The underpaid man becomes the physical and moral degenerate.

Note the conditions in the tenements and sweat shops of our cities, which are too well known to require comment. There are 20,000 such tenements in New York City alone in which abound disease, degradation and vice. Childhood is forced to contribute its uttermost to enrich able manufacturers.

Poverty is ugly and repellant everywhere, but when it assails the cradle it assumes its most hideous form. To the extent that children are robbed of their inherent right to laugh and be free, to the same extent do you cripple and blight society.

According to Professor Seager in his book, "The Bitter Cry of the Children," out of 171,732 deaths of children under five years of age in 1912, 78,263 were due to bad conditions and preventable. Appalling, and we maintain that nothing has been found so effective to prevent these sad conditions as the minimum wage. It is impossible to rear efficient, healthy and moral citizens in homes where the utmost wage of the father is insufficient to meet the needs of their frail bodies.

Human nature is selfish, and greed relentless, and as long as it is possible a certain class of unscrupulous employers will ever exploit labor.

Honorable Judges, does the fact that a man must toil justify an employer in taking an unfair advantage, to avail himself of labor half paid? No, eternally no.

Our opponents may contend that as a worker increases in efficiency in the same rate will his wages increase. This would be true if the pay check were always in the true proportion to the amount and efficiency of the labor performed. But what of the underpaid labor?

How can we expect the poor ignorant man, starving mentally and physically, wholly lacking in incentive and initiative, to rise above his present low level? A minimum wage by giving justice to all is the only remedy which does not at the same time destroy efficiency.

It will be argued that wages are governed by the law of supply and demand, but this law. in the words of Gide, the great French economist, is a blind law of a nature that has no regard for equality or justice. It does not take into consideration the fundamental principle does a laborer receive what he earns, but only is the supply so great that the laborer will be forced to accept whatever capital pleases to offer. Furthermore, the law cannot operate under abnormal conditions.

Then, since the law of supply is inefficient and unjust, a legal minimum based on principles of justice is needed to prevent great moral injury being inflicted on our nation. Is it any wonder that so much vice and crime exists, in view of the fact that not half of the women wage earners of the United States receive as much as $6 per week for their service? Furthermore, the death roll of the United States is greater than that of any other nation, due in large measure to industrial conditions. Because of the injury to the individual the state and public welfare must suffer for, be it known, the whole is no greater than the sum of its parts.

Honorable Judges, I have proven to you by government statistics that labor in many instances is underpaid in our country, whose fundamental principle is equal rights to all and special privilege to none.

I have proven that conditions demand a remedy, that we may stay the physical and moral degeneracy of our great laboring class, that their children may have the opportunity to develop into normal men and women, to compel the greedy, selfish employer to deal justly and fairly, to enable the mother to maintain her place in the home, not in the industrial world.

A remedy I say must be forthcoming, and what remedy shall we seek for, what so just and fair to all concerned as the minimum wage? In fact, I maintain that a minimum wage is necessary and essential to the physical and political life of the nation.

Legislation is the only effective means for bettering conditions, because, organization is impossible. Those who require the minimum wage are, as a class, incapable of exercising the administrative ability necessary for effective unionism. Organization among the employers is impossible, for the majority will not organize, and those who would can not. Again, legislation is the only means, for industrial education is too slow a process. Legislation is the only effective means for giving the people, who enter into wage contracts, equality before the law, and such a policy effectively operated by a wage board consisting of a fair representation of employers, employees and public opinion is the only means for making true, for the first time, that which has long been held to be true, that is, the establishment of just relations between employer and employee.

Now, ladies and gentlemen, in conclusion we rest the issue upon the fundamental principles involved and ultimate effects upon society, not upon the petty details. To recapitulate, we would not fix an arbitrary minimum based on the cost of living, but upon the capacity of the worker and profits of the industry. We contend merely for a wage as shall be just to both capital and labor. We recommend the adoption of a policy in a cautious manner, and in those industries where labor is most clearly exploited, and we shall insist that the negative team recognize and meet the problem of starvation wages in those industries.

Briefly, having given you our interpretation of a minimum wage, I have asserted and proven that immediate adoption of the policy in certain industries is necessary because of conditions that exist, and I have further proven that legislation is the only effective manner for controlling these conditions.

\*\*\*

Source: Inter-Collegiate Debate 1913-11914, of Baker University, edited by Geo. A Brown and F. W. Osterhout

A. R. Bradley, W. S. Davison, Ernest Reser
(from left to right)

\*\*\*

**John Bass, First Negative Speaker (Baker University)**

Honorable Judges, Ladies and Gentlemen: Before I take up the discussion for the negative I wish to call your attention to the argument set forth by my worthy opponent. His speech can be divided into two parts, in one portion he tried to picture the deplorable conditions as he saw them. In the other portion he paid a tribute to the minimum wage of Australia. My colleagues in the course of their argument will prove that the minimum wage in Australia has been an overwhelming failure, and should under no considerations be adopted in the United States.

The negative admit that the labor conditions in the United States are not what they should be; but we do not admit that they are as deplorable as my worthy opponent has pictured them. Honorable Judges, are we facing a crisis; are we plunging into an abyss of wreck and ruin owing to a few abnormal conditions in our laboring system?

Experience proves that we are not.

The Senate Investigating Committee of the Sixty-first Congress reports, that during the last seven years there has been an increase of eighteen per cent in the scale of wages and an eight percentage decrease in the length of working hours in forty-one of the leading industries. The labor report of the State of Conneticut states, that the average wage of women, exclusive of minors, was over $9.00 per week. The committee of the Kansas legislature that investigated the laboring conditions of this state, reports that every girl who was worth $9.00 per week is receiving $9-00. The 950 girls working in the Emery, Bird, Thayer Dry Goods Company of Kansas City, Mo., are receiving an average of $10.00 per week.

These facts go to prove, Ladies and Gentlemen, that the conditions are not as deplorable as my worthy opponent has so eloquently stated. The official organ of the American Federation of Labor says, "A great majority of our industries are paying more than a living wage to their employees, and where low wages are paid it is due to exceptional circumstances."

It is of these exceptional circumstances that I wish to speak.

The Negative maintain that the cause for low wages, which exists in a few industries cannot be remedied by minimum wage legislation.

My worthy opponent said if we maintain that the minimum wage cannot remedy the conditions of low wages, we must produce a better remedy.

Honorable Judges, it is not necessary for the negative to produce a better remedy.

The only thing we have to do is to prove the fallacies and defects of a minimum wage, and that is what we are going to do, beyond that we have no prerogative.

In considering the question of wages, we must consider those fundamental economic laws that underlie the whole theory of wages.

In the first place wages constitute the price paid for the service of labor, and hence come under the general law of supply and demand. This economic theory seems to be ignored by the advocates of a minimum wages, but the great authorities on economics like Tausig, Seager, Ely and Fetters, support the theory, that labor is controlled and regulated by the laws of supply and demand that are above any artificial laws that may be promulgated by the mind of man in a moment of restlessness.

How can a few men assembled in a state or national legislature establish laws to regulate a certain economic element, over which they have no control? The scale of wages will increase when the labor market is limited or restricted, in spite of the fact that men may legislate to the contrary. Any country has a high scale of wages when labor is scarce, but when its labor supply exceeds the demand as it does in some of the industries in the United States, the scale of wages will be low.

State regulation of wages is by no means a new thing. England tried it and failed, because the supply and demand of labor could not be regulated by acts of parliament. A certain school of economists set forth the reason, that because the police power of the state can enforce laws regulating the length of hours and unsanitary conditions, it can likewise regulate the rate of wages.

Such a hypothesis is wrong both in theory and in practice.

There are no economic laws regulating length of hours and unsanitary conditions to interfere with such legislation, but in the question of wages, between employer and employee, the economic laws plays a vital part and defies legislation.

Furthermore a minimum wage is not elastic, and cannot adjust itself to the ever fluctuating labor market. Suppose during the time of a commercial depression a large number of men are thrown out of employment, how could a minimum wage, established during a period of prosperity, adjust itself to the vast over supply of labor?

The price of labor in such a time would rapidly decrease, but the minimum wage being fixed by legislation would remain the same, in spite of adverse conditions. Therefore, because the minimum wage would seek to control labor which can only be controlled by economic laws; and that it would not be elastic in moments of depression, it is hailed by most students of economics as false in theory and dangerous in practice.

Now let us apply this economic law of supply and demand to the situation of labor in some of the lower industries. That there exists in some industries low wages, we admit, but at the same time there exists in these same industries an over supply of unskilled labor.

It is my purpose to prove that these conditions attributed to low wages are due primarily to the influx of unskilled and ignorant labor. The oversupply of labor is due to two causes:

First: Foreign immigration.
Second: The movement from the rural districts to the cities.

There are coming annually to our shores one and a quarter million immigrants, largely from Eastern and Southern Europe, who are ignorant of our customs and conditions. This class of unskilled and ignorant immigrants, because of their ability to endure long hours, and because of their low standards of life, have been the chief factor in bringing about the conditions that exist in the textile and sweated industries. The recent immigrants have little money when they arrive, and to avoid starvation they are forced to seek employment at any cost. About 75 per cent of the workers in the sweated industries are Southern and Eastern Europeans. This influx of foreign. immigration has so greatly exceeded the demand that today there exists a severe competition among the immigrants themselves, and these conditions in those industries have forced wages down to a very low standard.

The sweated industries did not exist prior to 1885. That year marks the coming of the Italians and Poles to our shores. They immediately congregated in the slums of our large cities; and owing to the severe competition among themselves for employment, they have brought about the conditions that exist in those industries.

The conditions in the textile industries of New England were very favorable, previous to the coming of the ignorant and illiterate immigrants from Southern Europe. The American workers in those industries were receiving good pay and working under favorable conditions, but the coming of the Europeans, with their low standards of living, so increased the supply of labor that the native Americans were forced to leave.

The foreigner today constitutes 80 per cent of the population in the industries where low wages are paid. Their ever increasing numbers and low standards of life are the chief causes for those conditions, and how is it possible to pass a law regulating low wages when those wages are caused by the nature of the individual?

In the second place our over supply of unskilled labor is due to the exodus from the rural districts to the cities. In 1890 the rural population constituted 72 per cent of the country's population; in

1910 it constituted 60 per cent. This decrease of the rural, and increase of urban population has had its effects upon the labor market.

The cotton manufacturers of the South have lured the poor white from their mountain homes to settle in the cities. This movement so greatly increased the supply of labor in the cotton factories that the child labor question has been the result.

That we have an over supply of unskilled labor is proved by experience. There were 3,000,000 out of employment in 1907. Last December, two months ago, the city council of Chicago passed a resolution asking the state to give them aid for 100,000 idle men.

Kansas City reported 50,000 idle men in 1911.

The inability to find employment is gathered by the department of labor at Washington which investigated the Italians in Chicago. It reports that the Italian is able to work on an average of only four months in the year owing to the great number of Italians in that city.

My opponent has quoted the average yearly wages of the employees in certain industries which on the face of it appears low. But remember that the amount he quoted is the wage they received for working a portion of the year. If the worker was able to work 52 weeks in the year his wage would have been at least four times that which my worthy opponent has quoted.

This overcrowded market of unskilled labor, caused by the influx of foreign immigration and movement from the rural districts into the city have been the causes of low wages. These conditions constitute the exceptional circumstance for the causes of low wages in some industries as mentioned by the organ of the American Federation of Labor.

Now the question is simply this. Can a minimum wage law eliminate these economic difficulties, decrease the number of unemployed and diminish the oversupply of unskilled labor? To accomplish that is the impossible, as mere legislation can not regulate nor control economic laws.

Now, Honorable Judges, since minimum wage legislation cannot eliminate the causes for low wages, why is such legislation agitated?

The first place we hear of modern minimum wage legislation is in Australia. It was agitated for political purposes. Australia today is considered the world's experiment ground for every form of freak legislation. It has no complicated commercial and industrial problem, and for that reason the people of that island spend their time in adopting every form of radical legislation. Every piece of social legislation today, whether good or bad, had its origin in Australia.

The minimum wage was advocated by the Socialist parts of Australia. This same party is now trying to regulate the cost of food products as attempting to regulate the price of a loaf of bread.

But what has been the success of the minimum wage in Australia?

McDonald, that noted English expert upon this subject, says: "If a minimum wage could have succeeded anywhere it would have been in Australia where they have tried various forms since 1894. The country is small, its industries simple; its population is but a handful and is not crowded into large cities; its industrial inspection is child's play, and it is protected by a high protective tariff.

But in spite of these favorable conditions, my colleague will prove that it has not been successful, and experience in that distant island would not justify its establishment in the United States. Mr. Aves and Clark were sent out by the English and American governments to investigate the minimum wage law in Australia. After two years of investigation they made a detailed report of their findings in which they warned their respective governments against its adoption.

The minimum wage was adopted by England in 1909 during the greatest strike in its history. Coming to America, it was passed in Massachusetts in 1912 during the period of the Lawrence strike.

Both employer and employee were opposed to this law, but in spite of their opposition it was passed by unscrupulous politicians and urged upon the non-interested voter. Mr. McSweeny, a member of the Massachusetts Industrial Board, said:

"The so-called minimum wage law which went into effect July 1, 1913, is a monument to the timidity of the Massachusetts legislature which allowed itself to be bullied into passing without debate, a bill not for the sake of humanity, but for the fear that the failure to pass it might cost them votes."

An investigation shows that the best economic students of our day are opposed to minimum wage legislation. President Wilson and Dr. Hadley of Yale are among its opponents. As a whole both American capital and labor are opposed to it. Both organized and unorganized labor have repudiated and denounced minimum wage legislation.

Mr. Gompers, the most influential labor leader in the United States, in voicing the sentiment of the American Federation of Labor, says:

"We must not, we cannot depend upon legislative enactments to set wage standards." During the agitation for minimum wage legislation in California the working women of that state sent eight representatives to their legislature who bitterly opposed the minimum wage law.

About a year ago our legislature voted down the minimum wage law, and when the bill was under consideration, petitions were sent to the legislature signed by thousands of Kansas working girls requesting the legislature to defeat the measure for the sake of their pride and interest. Since both the employer and employee are opposed to it, what reasons are there for its adoption in the United States.

In conclusion, I have proved: First, that labor is controlled by economic laws and not by legislation.

Second: Low wages, where they exist, are due to the conditions of labor market and cannot be remedied by a minimum wage law.

Third: That both the employer and employee are opposed to it.

For these reasons we maintain that a minimum wage should not be put into operation in the United States.

Bass, Brown, & Osterhout

(from Left to Right)

## Glossary of Terms

• Adjudicator – The judge(s) of the debate.
• Argumentation – The act or process of forming reasons and evidence to support your case.
• Audibility – Speaking loud enough to be heard in all parts of the room.
• Authority – Knowing your facts and figures, using expert sources.
• Ballot – The judge(s) vote(s) for the team which they think won the debate.
• Conviction – Belief in, and concern for, the topic you are talking about.
• Delivery – The way a speaker speaks, the speaking style. It is both verbal and nonverbal.
• Engagement – Keeping the attention of the audience.
• Flowing – Taking notes in a debate.
• Likability – A pleasing, well-mannered, nice person who is courteous and respectful.
• Motion – The topic of the debate.
• Opposition team – The negative team.
• Point of Information (POI) – A question about something the speaker said (or didn't say).
• Proposition team – The affirmative team.
• Rebuttal – Finding fault with the arguments the other team has made.
• Status quo – The way things are now.
• Team line – A phrase or sentence used by all speakers on a team to finish their speech.
• Team split – The division of labor, how a team has divided their case among its speakers.

• Summary Speech / Reply Speech – The final speech for a team.
• WSDC – World Schools Debating Championship (International Competition).

---

# ABOUT THE AUTHOR

Thomas Baker is the Past-President of TESOL Chile (2010-2011). He is the Coordinator of the English Department at Colegio Internacional SEK in Santiago, Chile.

He is the Co-Founder and Co-Organiser of EdCamp Santiago: free, participant-driven, democratic, conversation based professional development for teachers, by teachers. EdCamp Santiago 2013 was held at Universidad UCINF in Santiago.

Thomas is also a past member of the Advisory Board for the International Higher Education Teaching and Learning Association (HETL), where he also serves as a reviewer and as the HETL Ambassador for Chile.

http://goo.gl/qYo8BH

Thomas enjoys writing about a wide variety of topics. He has written the following genres: romance, historical fiction, autobiographical, sports history/biography, and English Language Teaching.

http://goo.gl/mdU4iG

http://www.profesorbaker.com

email: profesorbaker@gmail.com

Twitter: @profesortbaker

Made in the USA
Monee, IL
08 January 2020